S0-BAK-220

# NEW SPACES, OLD WORLD CHARM

## THE ART OF ELEGANT INTERIORS

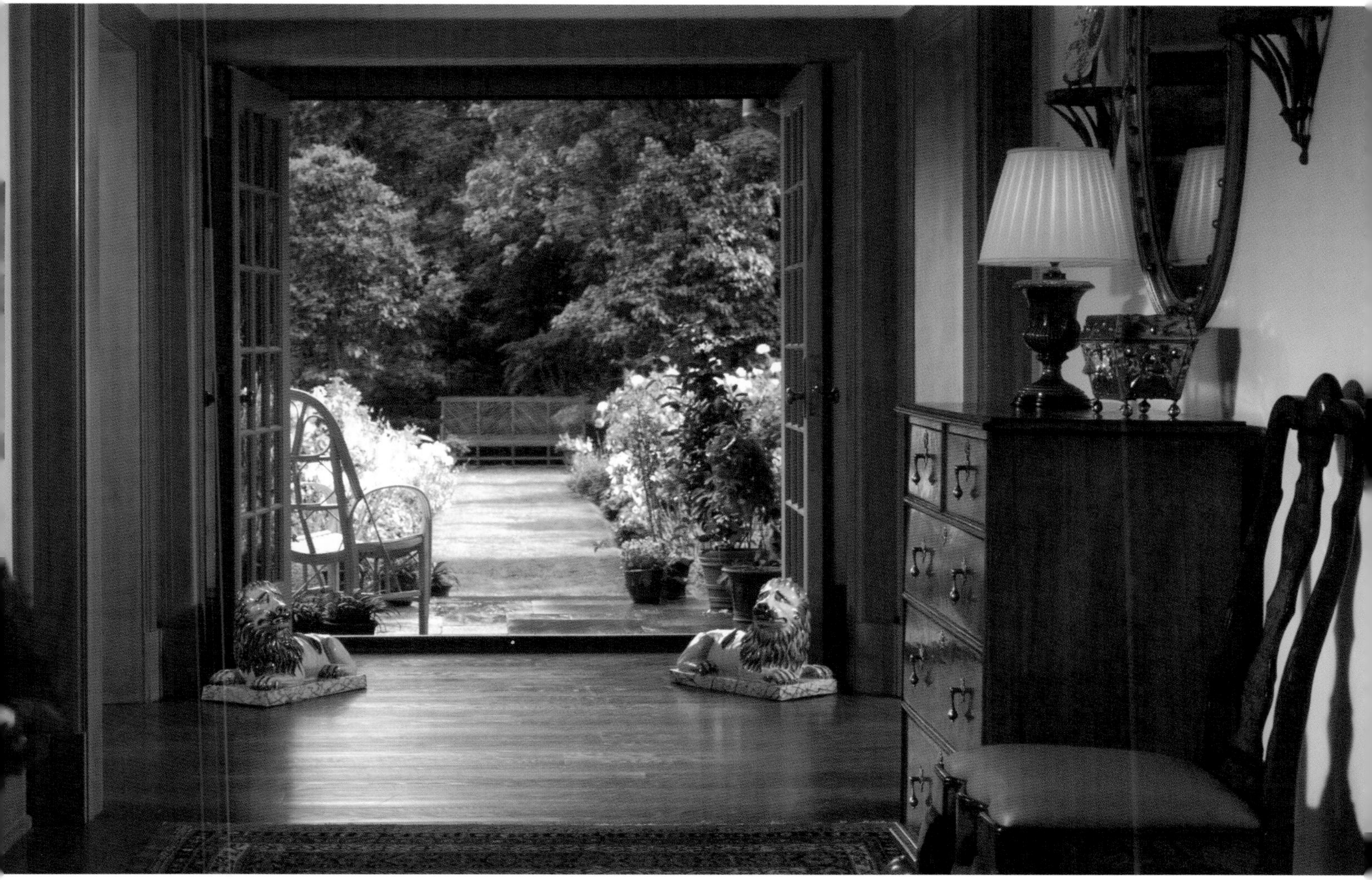

Ann Sample

Forward by Robert Couturier

The McGraw-Hill Companies

Cataloging-in-Publication Data is on file with the Library of Congress



1 2 3 4 5 6 7 8 9 0 PUR/PUR 0 1 0 9 8 7 6 5

ISBN 0-07-143929-3.

The sponsoring editor for this book was Cary Sullivan and the production supervisor was Pamela Pelton.

Printed in China by Print Vision.

McGraw-Hill books are available at special quantity discounts to use as premiums and sales promotions, or for use in corporate training programs. For more information, please write to the Director of Special Sales, McGraw-Hill, 2 Penn Plaza, New York, NY 10121-2298. Or contact your local bookstore.

The book is printed on acid-free stock.

Information contained in this book has been obtained by The McGraw-Hill Companies, Inc. ("McGraw-Hill"), from sources believed to be reliable. However, neither McGraw-Hill nor its authors guarantee the accuracy or completeness of any information published herein, and neither McGraw-Hill nor its authors shall be responsible for any errors, omissions or damages arising out of use of this information. This work is published with the understanding that McGraw-Hill and its authors are supplying information, but are not attempting to render engineering or other professional services. If such services are required, the assistance of an appropriate professional should be sought.

Packaged by Elements Media
Creative Director: Chris Kincade
Art Direction/Graphic Design: Boomerang Studio
Editorial Assistant: Gayle Brosnan

Elements of Living is a trademark of Elements Media, LLC.

Elements Media, LLC
16 West 19th Street, Tenth Floor
New York, NY 10011

# DEDICATION

For A.L.L, C.L. and P.R.D.


# ACKNOWLEDGEMENTS

I would like to first acknowledge the interior designers, architects, artisans, photographers and other sources who participated in this book. It has been an honor and a joy getting to know each of you. I appreciate all the time you gave me, with special thanks to Robert Couturier, Carl D'Aquino, Scott Salvator, Glenn Gissler, Ellie Cullman, Ira Grandberg, Joe Nahem and Laura Resen. I am equally indebted to Cary Sullivan, my editor at McGraw-Hill, Chris Kincade of Elements Media and Inge Heckel of The New York School of Interior Design for championing my project, as well as to Gayle Brosnan of Elements Media for her enthusiastic help throughout the writing, photo-gathering and editing processes. Additional thanks to my family and friends, especially my devoted mother, Kathleen Sample, for sharing her love of books with me and my loving husband, Christopher Lineberger, who always encourages me to pursue what makes me happy. Lastly, being a new mom, I could not have written this book without the dedication of my daughter's babysitter, Lucy Rairan, as well as my husband.


Dear Tamara,
I hope you enjoy reading my book and find it inspirational.
Best wishes,
Ann

# TABLE OF CONTENTS

# FOREWORD

## BY ROBERT COUTURIER

"Old World" has not always meant cozy and charming. In their day, our grandmothers were likely dreaming of vacuum cleaners, dishwashers and washing machines. They burned their hands while cooking over an open flame, cleaned with nothing more than a broom, washed clothes by hand in running cold water and made their own candles and soap, as shopping usually required a day-long journey on foot. I doubt that they delighted in getting their heat from wood they had to chop from tree trunks!

Their homes, too, were designed with an emphasis on practicality. Architectural details were a necessity—nothing was created solely for aesthetic purposes. There were few gratuitous details, and beauty and refinement were the privilege of less than one percent of the population. Craftsmanship was reserved for a very few.

Trying to recreate an old world look, in fact, is a very new concept. If you look at historic design periods, you'll realize that every home was furnished in contemporary styles. So even as you commit to an *old world* sense of craft, take the idea of its charm with a grain of salt. Don't take it too seriously and try to have fun. Too many cozy antique elements, such as cooking utensils or spinning wheels, can make a room look overly quaint and a bit silly. Emphasizing the past at the expense of invention leads to old-fashioned, outdated spaces better left in museums—or worse, to Disneyland recreations.

Elegant spaces inspired by the past are successful when they respect sacred proportions. Everything that was built until the last few decades incorporated one of four different orders: Doric, Ionic, Corinthian or composite. When you add old world architectural details, such as columns or pillars, without considering these elements, the result lacks an appropriate sense of proportion. So if you want your home to look authentic, don't add moldings just to add moldings; make sure that they are in perfect balance with the other architectural elements.

Above all, remember that whatever you choose to do must not only come from the heart, but also have a respect for and knowledge of the culture or design period that serves as your inspiration. No matter what, old world charm will always be something of an illusion. The projects profiled here have it because they mix a reverence for the past with a spirit of discovery!

Couturier's designs reflect his European background. They are high-minded, worldly and adventuresome; eclectic in the truest sense of the word.

OCEANLIFE

INTRODUCTION

# DISCOVERING NEW WORLD CHARM

Fluted pilasters and plaster moldings, exposed beams and fieldstone fireplaces, Delft tiles and wide oak planks—aren't antique home details evocative? They call to mind a time when houses were built with exquisitely handcrafted details, long before suburban developments and cookie-cutter homes became common. In that era, families carefully designed their homes or hired classically trained architects to do so for them. Today's building methods just don't come close to duplicating the enchanting elements of older homes.

But, sadly, for every delightful detail of an antique home, there are several age-related problems. Older homes have dated utility systems, appliances and floor plans, while newly constructed homes simply come with rooms built to meet today's lifestyle needs and fewer expensive "surprises."

And therein lies the problem. Most people want the ease and comfort of new homes, but appreciate the details of older ones. *New Spaces, Old World Charm* offers a simple solution, showing you how to turn new, unadorned rooms into history-laden interiors. It follows 14 masters of the new-to-old transformation as they develop their own projects, often building a home from scratch or fully gutting and redesigning what's already there. These celebrated interior designers and architects work in a wide variety of styles, but they all specialize in creating timeless, vintage spaces.

Each chapter offers an in-depth look at the designer's work, demonstrating how he or she incorporates historical styles, classic design principles and his or her own unique concepts into an antique take on contemporary rooms.

*New Spaces, Old World Charm* is not a book about historic recreations. As designer Carl D'Aquino says, "My rooms are grounded in history, but I never want them to be so enslaved to a style that they look like they belong in a museum." Rather, each featured space shows how to create innovative and exciting interiors by combining and updating period details and furnishings. Ann LeConey, for example, relied on five different styles to design a Palm Beach home, while Glenn Gissler mixed rustic Colonial and Third World furniture and artifacts within a Shaker-inspired framework.

In reading *New Spaces, Old World Charm*, you'll discover that there is a science to the instant antique, and it's one that you can learn. Despite stylistic differences, all of the designers rely on similar techniques. Some use bold colors to make oversized rooms feel more intimate, while others enliven plain walls by adding paneling, molding and built-ins. Some use hand-painted, romantic landscape murals to evoke an earlier era, while others install salvaged architectural elements to lend rooms the look of age. Above all, every designer uses eclectic furniture arrangements to make new spaces feel like they have evolved over generations. (To make the new-to-old process even easier to understand, a selection of designer tips accompany each chapter.)

Finding the right resources is a big part of the transformation. To help get you started, *New Spaces, Old World Charm* includes over 145 of the featured designers' favorite sources, including the artisans they hire to achieve their old world effects. The section on reproduction furniture lists more than

Masters of the new-to-old transformation: **Top row, left to right**, Ann LeConey, Carl D'Aquino and Francine Monaco, David Chu, Peter Chu, Elissa Cullman, Ira Grandberg. **Bottom row, left to right**, Glenn Gissler, Jack Phillips, Randy Ridless, Robert Couturier, Scott Salvator, Joe Nahem and Tom Fox. Not Pictured: Anthony Ingrao and Steven Gambrel.

10 celebrity designers who produce their own furnishings. Another section includes designers' favorite antiques stores, most of which are accessible over the Internet. Other sources range from manufacturers of high-quality, historically inspired textiles to vintage-styled plumbing vendors to hardware retailers to architectural salvage shops. (It should be noted that these sources are a combination of trade and retail, ranging from high-end to budget. If you're not working with a designer, you may be able to use a buying service to purchase trade-only products. Look for one in the trade tips section (page 182), or call local design centers to find similar services.)

The artisans profiled vary from painters to lighting designers to furniture refinishers, all of them masters of their crafts. Throughout the resource sections, the designers share additional tips, such as how to upholster furniture, avoid predictability in traditional décor and use light fixtures to add character to new spaces. I think you'll find these sections to be of invaluable assistance. (For related resources, see *Elements of Living* magazine, which lists the top contacts for a wide array of furnishings; issues are available at major bookstores and subscriptions at www.elementsofliving.com.)

My hope is that *New Spaces, Old World Charm* will convince you that it's possible to create the character-rich rooms you admire in your own newly built or remodeled home. Let it inspire you to redecorate, keep building, or design from scratch. Whatever the project, this book is meant as an illustrative guide to developing spaces with history, style and comfort. In short, places that feel like home.

D'AQUINO & MONACO



# CHAPTER 1

# UPDATED COLONIAL

When homeowners need to transform a brand new box into a home with roots, they call on Carl D'Aquino and Francine Monaco, of the Manhattan-based design firm D'Aquino Monaco. For a new Connecticut home that resembled Mount Vernon on the outside and a 20th-century builder's home on the inside, the duo designed an interior with a history as rich as its exterior demanded. After a fire ravaged a Victorian home, they recreated the architectural elements and then updated its interior style to give it a modern flair. And in home after home, D'Aquino and Monaco have come up with innovative ways to eliminate "newness" from freshly-built rooms.

In business for over 20 years, D'Aquino studied to become an architect, but ultimately decided interior design was his greater passion. Monaco is a practicing architect who also teaches her craft at New York's Pratt Institute of Art and Design. Their combined architectural knowledge and training in the classics gives this team the breadth of experience needed to successfully tackle whatever style their clients desire, from Colonial to mid-century modern. As a result, their signature look is not tied to a particular period, but rather demonstrates an ability to give new spaces the patina of age—while still incorporating bold, brash colors into fresh, stylish designs.

When you mention "builders' homes" to D'Aquino, his pained expression quickly indicates how many headaches they have caused him over the years.

**Opposite:** This massive two-story foyer appears to be large enough to double as a chopper landing. To tame the voluminous space, D'Aquino oversized everything, from the diamond pattern on the floor and the stripes on the wall, to the chandelier and furniture. If all elements in a large space are equally large the room will seem more balanced.

**Above:** The 18th-century harbor scene references the home's main design theme of a ship captain who sailed around the world and brought back pieces of furniture from each port. The mural was painted on the main stairwell by artisans Marguerite MacFarlane and Peter Cozzolino so that it would greets visitors at the front door.

"There are several problems with builders' homes," he says. "The biggest one is scale.

"In an attempt to make a grand statement, developers often build absolutely huge homes with cathedral ceilings. They are trying to mimic some of the great homes of Europe, but their floor plans, scale and cheap design materials just don't give the desired effect. It is then the designer's job to transform the huge spaces into approachable, friendly and warm rooms."

D'Aquino and Monaco recently encountered such a challenge when a longtime client approached them to design the interiors of her brand new, 30,000 square-foot house in New Jersey. Although both she and her husband are retired, and live alone, they had built a home large enough to accommodate their eight grown children and their children's families. Given the large number of potential visitors to the house, the project's scale initially seemed daunting. "The only word I could come up with as I toured my client's new home was 'humongous,'" says D'Aquino. "I panicked. I asked myself, 'How can I possibly do something with these rooms so that they can be at a scale to be enjoyed?' "

## Masters of Invention

D'Aquino and Monaco's first step was devising a theme. "When we start a new project, we start with the thread of a story—and over time, the entire story evolves," D'Aquino says, explaining that he and Monaco develop a design "narrative" to guide their work. The inspiration, he continues, "can be a specific type of person, like an antique dealer specializing in Arts and Crafts, or a piece of art, such as a Piet Mondrian painting. As the planning process progresses, the story unfolds."

For this home, D'Aquino, Monaco and their client

decided that a worldly 18th-century ship captain would be the inspiration for their design decisions. Thus, all the furniture and decorative elements in the house needed to be items their fictitious sailor might have brought back from his travels. It was decided that they had to be antiques or reproductions of pieces from the 1700s or earlier (though they could come from any part of the world). Continuing on this theme, D'Aquino and Monaco adapted traditional Colonial architectural details to fit the home's scale and commissioned antique-looking murals of seaports for its walls.

**Opposite Bottom:** The windows in the home are massive in comparison to those found in traditional Colonial dwellings. In the library, D'Aquino and Monaco added suitably large marble busts that filled the spaces and disguised their size, while lending a decidedly historic note.

## Oversized Challenges, Colorful Solutions

Although their ingenious theme gave the project the eclecticism it needed, D'Aquino, Monaco and their client still had to address the problem of scale. To make the rooms feel more livable, the team used strong color, fabrics with large, repeating patterns, and oversized architectural elements, furniture and decorative accessories.

The color scheme dramatically softened the scale of the interiors. The three collaborators then settled on a series of bold hues for the majority of the rooms, with as much blue

**Above:** The library mimics the foyer in shape and size, with a matching second-story balcony. Since this room opens off the entranceway, the deep porcelain blue seen in the foyer's stripes was repeated to allow for a smooth transition between the two areas. The color also creates a sense of warmth in both rooms.

DESIGNER TIPS

**Allow a Story to Guide the Design:** Inspiration can be derived from virtually anywhere: a historical era, a person, a song—even a poem. As you design, let the story unfold to create a rich, layered scheme. If you pick an aesthitic period, be sure to add elements from other eras so that the design of your home is not predictable.

**Consider a Progression of Color:** Rather than painting all the walls in one color scheme, D'Aquino and Monaco spice things up with color sequences that feature complementary but different hues. Start your color sequence at the foyer and end in the kitchen. It will delight your guests as they move through your home, and mediate the scale of the rooms.

**Use Strong Color Schemes:** Many of us are afraid vibrant colors will overpower a space, but because they help set the mood and add period details, they can effectively counter the newness of a house. If you're unsure about your color choices, paint a wide section on the wall (at least 5' by 5'), place furniture in front of it and check it throughout the day, as the light changes.

**Add Traditional Architectural Elements:** In large scale rooms, large architectural details disguise the scale. Install paneling, moldings, built-in cabinets, fireplace surrounds and coffered, timbered or beamed ceilings. Have these details custom-made or install salvaged pieces from homes set to be demolished. (Local antiques stores often sell salvaged architectural details or can send you to the proper source.)

The paint color in this traditional Colonial dining room was inspired by a house in historic Mount Vernon. The secondary color, fuchsia, injects a burst of vitality. The room looks period but the informal gingham fabric and the mating of pink with traditional Colonial blue-green is a refreshing twist on early American design.

(the client's favorite color) as possible. D'Aquino was thrilled to work for someone who shared his appreciation of vibrant color schemes. "Color is a way to defeat the newness of a house because it sets a mood and a tone, and can be used to add a period note," he says. "And strong color tricks the eye and makes the walls appear to come forward. Color can make even the largest room feel intimate."

D'Aquino and Monaco also used the classic design technique of color progression to draw people from one space to the next. "You are gently pulled through this house by the color sequence," D'Aquino says. "There is an evolution of color that begins with the boldness of the two tones of the entry's blue, and continues through the rich blue-green of the dining room into the soothing pastels of the living room and beyond. As you move through the home, you want to know more. At the same time, this mix of complementary but different colors takes the focus off the rooms' scale."

Another essential component of this home's new-to-old transformation is the extensive use of period architectural elements. "The walls were either plain gypsum board or were littered with inappropriately-scaled moldings and chair railings," says D'Aquino. "We replaced the existing moldings with custom–made ones, paneled some of the rooms, added built-ins and dressed the fireplaces to look like they belonged to a fine 18th-century Colonial house." Not all of the architectural elements installed in the home were new, though: Some were recovered from aging buildings set to be demolished. "Installing real antique architectural elements is one sure way to give a new home a sense of history," the designer says.

Murals depicting antique scenes were added to give the home a sense of history. D'Aquino hired artisans to paint an

D'Aquino and Monaco used a progression of color in this home, moving from dark to light. Located at the end of that spectrum, the living room departs in color from the other first-floor rooms, offering a calm respite. Its hues are much more serene, tending toward cream, raspberry, pale yellow and pink. Although more muted in color, the room is still in keeping with the 18th-century style of the rest of the home.

This island dominates a large country-style kitchen. Big enough to double as a buffet, it is multileveled so that both adults and kids can join in meal preparation. An 18th-century pastoral scene enlivens the walls and makes for a great conversation piece.

"Color is a way to defeat the newness of a house because it sets a mood and a tone, and can be used to add a period note."

18th-century seaport scene in the kitchen and foyer. The kitchen's mural runs around the entire room and nicely complements the space's salvaged architectural elements. The other mural was painted on the foyer stairway's risers—literally running up the stairs—and can be seen as one enters the front door. "Of all the elements in the house, the murals are the best at instantly representing the owners' desire for their just-built home to look as if it was owned by a ship captain," D'Aquino says. "We wanted one of the murals to meet people at the front door as a way to set the stage for the rest of the home."

The informal dining area of the country kitchen has a Colonial-inspired custom-made bench. It is elongated to match the size of the large table positioned in front of it, but despite being supersized, still retains an antique flavor due to its design and paint color.

In the bedroom suite, D'Aquino and Monaco used a red and neutral palette. The vine crewel pattern on the bedspread and canopy is slightly outsized, which suits the large scale of the room and its furniture. The pine shutters adorning the windows further add to the country Colonial room scheme.

**Add Murals for Interest:** Hire an artist to paint historic murals on walls to add an intstant period note. Antique print books or illustrated ones can spur ideas, and depending on the location of your home, you can choose seaside, pastoral or urban landscapes. (If you're on a budget, you can also buy mural-like wallpaper.)

**Match Furnishings to the Period:** Fill your house with antiques or antique reproductions from the periods of design you are imitating. If you can't find what you need or the pieces are prohibitively expensive, hire a furniture maker to duplicate favorite pieces from pictures or detailed drawings.

**Match Furnishings to the Scale:** If some of the rooms feel too large for the furniture you already own, replace a few of the dominant items—a sofa, armoire or bed, perhaps—with larger scale pieces and mix the new items with your other existing furniture.

**Soften Scale with Patterns:** When upholstering larger scale pieces of furniture, choose fabrics solid in color or with larger patterns, so that the two elements work well together once joined. A small pattern on a large sofa or chair only amplifies the size of the piece of furniture. Remember that everything in a room needs to be in scale. If the room is large, the other major elements of the room need to match proportionally.

## Decorative Touches

Once the "interior shell" of the house looked authentically antique, the design team began filling the couple's home with furniture and other decorative elements from the 18th century, gathering objects from many corners of the earth. "We wanted every room to appear as if the captain had sailed to England, Europe, Ireland and other spots and acquired a few possessions in each country," says D'Aquino. Like so many other elements acquired for the project, the antiques are larger than the norm. "Oversized pieces bring the room's scale into manageable proportions," the designer explains. "It's another visual trick. You pick slightly bigger furniture pieces to suit the larger scale of the rooms." In this case, whatever furniture could not be bought was custom-built based on the firm's designs.

Following this bigger-is-better approach, the fabrics chosen for the house were designed with large patterns. D'Aquino says this is vital when large pieces of furniture are to be upholstered. "In this home, I used patterns that look amplified in comparison to those typically seen," he notes. "The larger scale of the fabric tricks the eye into perceiving the furniture and the entire space to be smaller than it is."

As in all of the homes the team designs, decorative accessories added the final touch, with an emphasis on oversized items such as antique prints, sconces and vases. One group of accessories, however, was purposely *not* oversized—the furniture and toys meant to appeal to the client's many grandchildren. D'Aquino and Monaco's firm placed an antique toddler's chair in each of the public rooms, and bought antique toys and kid-sized desks for many of the guestrooms.

"After oversizing so much of the house, it was a great joy to put something so tiny in such a large space," D'Aquino says. "Adults absolutely melt when they see children's furniture, and having it in all the rooms of the house makes the grandkids feel welcome."

The home's exaggerated proportions, colors and themes at play in the design of the home are not immediately apparent to its many guests because they are executed so consistently and masterfully. "The progression of color in the separate rooms of the house—from bold blue to soothing pastels—draws people in while distracting them from the overall scale," D'Aquino says. "That, along with pumped-up architectural details, furniture and textile designs, is what defeats the rooms' once-impersonal scale and brings the entire house into proper proportion."

A detail of the bed's upholstered headboard and curtains shows how to successfully mate an ancient crewel pattern and a modern geometric one.

# REPRODUCTION FURNITURE

1.

*Given that designers have an eye for buying antiques and are frequently antiquarians, it makes sense that they would be talented at designing reproductions. Some designers, such as John Rosselli, sell their designs through their own shops, mixed in among the antiques; others, including Michael Smith, sell largely to their well-heeled clients. And then there are the more commercially oriented (a.k.a. Martha Stewart), who sign on with major furniture manufacturers and have them produce their lines. The following is a list of interior designers and other design-oriented people who are responsible for some of the best reproductions on the market.*

2.

**BILL SOFIELD:** 1,2
The co-founder of famed design firm AERO Studios, Bill Sofield has a line of Baker furniture that mixes traditional style with modern flair. His handsome pieces are clean and sophisticated, often with squared-off lines. There is no one historical reference; some pieces have Asian influences, while others seem to be inspired by Napoleon's Empire period. Sofield has put a new spin on antique furniture, creating pieces that are familiar in form but novel in overall design. His furnishings are suitable for both traditional and contemporary settings. Retail. **Visit www.kohler.com.**

3.

**ROBERT KUO:** 3
Robert Kuo's line of limited-edition furniture for McGuire is truly a work of art. Using some of the world's finest materials, and relying on centuries-old artisanal techniques, this skilled artist has created 30 jewel-like pieces. Some are made from reclaimed, indigenous Chinese wood, which gives them an instantly old look; all depend on ancient building methods, including mortise-and-tenon joinery. For decoration, Kuo hand-hammers reliefs and applies lacquer using a 6,000-year-old method. The furniture's clean lines further serve to highlight its depth and complexity. Retail. **Visit www.kohler.com.**

**BARBARA BERRY:** 4
L.A.-based designer Barbara Berry is renowned for her simple, modern, feminine style—and her two furniture lines for Kohler's Baker and McGuire embody that aesthetic. The pieces are as glamorous as they are luxurious, with clean lines

and rich materials that remind one of 1930s Art Deco pieces, but with a more modern sensibility. Baker's line is largely composed of dark wood, gilded, and upholstered pieces, while McGuire's line is generally made from the company's signature material—rattan—and also includes upholstered pieces. Both lines are equally elegant. Retail. **Visit www.kohler.com.**

4.

**FRANCES MAYES:** 5, 6, 7
Although author Frances Mayes (*Under the Tuscan Sun*, Chronicle Books, 1996) is not an interior designer, she is known as an expert on Italy and its lifestyle. So when she recently approached Drexel Heritage and asked if she could lend her expertise to a line of Tuscan-inspired furniture, the company agreed. The line of 50 pieces, which Mayes calls "organic but romantic," ranges from wine cabinets (of course!) to beds, and is available in an array of finishes. The fabrics that adorn the upholstered pieces are made in Italy by a sixth-generation textile manufacturer, and all of the furniture is based on antiques Mayes discovered in Tuscany's countryside (some of which she currently owns). Available through various U.S. retailers. **Visit www.drexelheritage.com.**

5.

**JOHN ROSELLI**
John Rosselli conducts business in a three-story Manhattan building brimming with furniture and *objets d'art*. But the famed designer has several U.S. locations, including a venue in Washington, D.C. It's no wonder he's in demand: Top designers have been going to Rosselli for furniture since the 1950s, lured by his consummate skill and a now storied career that began with his hand-painting pieces for legendary designers Sister Parish, Billy Baldwin and Dorothy Draper. Despite being an antiquarian, Rosselli never lets his own designs look too academic or staid: He creates and sells items that are as whimsical as they are beautiful. His shops offer English, American and Continental antiques (including porcelain and ceramics), as well as reproduction furniture, lighting and upholstery fabrics (including originals and Robert Kime textiles). Retail and To the Trade showrooms. **Call 212-772-2137**

6.

7.

1.

2.

3.

**MARTHA STEWART**

Like so many of her products, Martha Stewart's line of furniture has its roots in traditional design, but is updated in a refreshing style. She enlivens staid Windsor chairs by making them from aluminum (with an antique pewter finish), turns an old fashion map table into a coffee table, and offers wing chairs in a decidedly non-traditional solid taupe. Produced by Bernhardt furniture, Stewart's three lines—Lily Pond, Skylands and Turkey Hill—total about 350 pieces. Their only common theme? Americana. Available through various U.S. retailers. **Visit www.marthastewart.com.**

**MICHAEL S. SMITH**

Serving Hollywood's in-crowd, California-based Michael S. Smith was recently named *Elle Décor*'s Designer of the Year. His reproduction furniture is starting to get the same sort of attention: In six years, he has created 85 expertly crafted, antique-looking pieces. His secret? Master craftspeople recreate his favorite vintage furnishings. Smith's line ranges from early-19th century Italian to mid-century modern; a catalog is available. Retail. **Call: 310-315-3018**

**RANDY RIDLESS:** 1

Constantly included in design magazines' Top 100 lists, Randy Ridless is known for his glamorous commercial interiors. He is the man responsible for the design of all Burberry stores, as well as the gorgeous new first and second floors at Manhattan's Bergdorf Goodman. Last fall, he began to sell his pieces (once only available to clients) to a wider audience. Classic, yet elegantly updated, they feature rich materials such as Macassar ebony, Lucite and suede. For more information on Ridless, turn to Chapter 11, *Traditional Redefined*. To the Trade. **Call 212-643-8140**

4.

**JULIA GRAY:** 2

As a designer, Julia Gray once worked for a variety of high-end furniture retailers. But in 1987, she decided to start her own firm, selling antiques acquired on trips to Europe. Two years after that, she also launched a line of hand-painted reproduction furniture, inspired by 18th-century styles. Her designs are as beautiful as the antiques she sells—and many are customized to suit modern lifestyles. To control the quality of her line, Gray founded her own workshop, where all of the finishes are applied. There are now 150 Julia Gray reproduction items, ranging from armoires to beds and small side tables. Her most exceptional pieces are made of satinwood, designed in restrained (but elegant) Edwardian style. To the Trade. **Call 212-223-4454.**

5.

6.

**OSCAR DE LA RENTA:** 3, 4, 5, 6

In late 2002, Oscar de la Renta introduced a line of furniture for Century, and it has been creating a stir ever since. His collection is divided into three groups, each inspired by a very different locale: Manhattan, Connecticut and Punta Cana, in the Dominican Republic. Styles ranges from sophisticated urban to country suburban and tropical vacation home—but one piece really stands out: The clever, round Radial Expansion table, based on a 19th-century design, which has eight leaves and expands from 60 to 84 inches in diameter. Retail. **Visit www.centuryfurniture.com**

7.

**THOMAS PHEASANT:** 7, 8

Thomas Pheasant's line of furniture was introduced by Baker nearly 10 years ago. Since then, the celebrated designer's collection has grown to over 30 pieces, all of which have a disciplined elegance and a symmetrical, neoclassic style. Pheasant's wooden furniture generally has straight, masculine lines, which nicely complements his curvy, tufted, upholstered pieces. A striking Constellation Mirror is among the most recognizable items: Its rays radiate out from the center. Retail. **Visit: www.kohler.com**

8.

JOE NAHEM

CHAPTER 2

# URBAN SOPHISTICATION

It is often said that Joe Nahem is the designer to call when you want Chanel with combat boots. In other words: pure luxury tempered with a bit of funk. Like his varied list of clients, Nahem's design work is a diverse mix. For every chic Manhattan residence he has designed, there is an equally compelling rustic beach house or Americana-themed farmhouse. The thread that runs through all of his work is the designer's sense of innovation—his rooms are as novel as they are inviting.

In April 2003, after he had been in business for almost 20 years, Nahem lost his partner, Tom Fox, and an associate, Michael Campanelli, to a plane crash that occurred on route to a design site. As a tribute to Fox and Campanelli, the residence profiled in this chpater is a collaborative effort between the three men, as well as other associates at the firm, Architect Thomas Vail and Focus Lighting, a lighting consultant. Nahem is now the sole partner of Fox-Nahem.

To create intriguing environments full of old world details, Nahem, who studied interior design at Manhattan's Parsons School of Design, relies on a variety of tools. His signatures include classic-yet-understated architectural elements, unique antiques, custom-designed upholstered furniture, vintage fabrics and outstanding hardware and light fixtures. Although rooted in the past, Nahem's work is marked by exciting juxtapositions of old and new—and his rooms are

**Opposite:** Nahem specializes in character-rich rooms with a generous dose of funk.

rarely anchored in just one historic style.

## A Fashionable, Historic Rehab

The residence in this chapter is a case in point. Normally, a Stanford White-designed townhouse wouldn't qualify for a "new space" makeover. White was a founding partner of McKim, Mead and White, the legendary Manhattan-based architectural firm. During the 19th and early 20th centuries, the firm designed extravagant palazzos for upscale families such as the Pulitzers and Whitneys. This brick Neo-Federal

**Above:** To infuse his new homes with the flavor of something vintage, Nahem gravitates towards striking light fixtures, such as this early 20th-century metal and seeded glass lantern. **Right:** This brown leather banquette lends the kitchen the feeling of a 1950s diner.

*"The* ***French plaster*** *we used looks like a* ***fresco****. There is such* ***depth*** *and* ***beauty*** *to it. The best faux painter couldn't duplicate its effect on sheetrock walls."*

home, however, was designed in 1904 for White's personal friend, artist and "Gibson Girl" creator Charles Dana Gibson. The artist was not as wealthy as a typical White client and his home was built with more modest materials.

When Nahem first saw the house, it practically begged for an infusion of old world charm, having served as an office space for the previous 50 years. The seven-story, 22-foot-wide townhouse was literally a collection of cubicles. Other than the stairway banister, a few of the Robert Adams-inspired fireplace mantels and the dining room's simple paneling, most of the original White details had already been removed. "Although there was not much of White's design left when our clients bought the townhouse, the overall design was more modern-looking than other White spaces because of the original client's limited budget and a lack of flourish and rich materials," says Nahem. "That is what appealed to our clients, along with the home's good bones and the abundance of natural light."

The clients liked the idea of owning a White-designed property, but were not interested in a line-by-line restoration of the original home—nor did they want to live in a typical Upper East Side townhouse. As a result, Nahem says, the home's design became a balance between architecture and cosmetics. "The clients wanted to respect the original structure, but the townhouse's overall design had to be glamorous," says Nahem.

While the clients wanted a gracious yet glamorous home, they didn't want a space that felt *too* grand. They insisted that every floor in the house be equally friendly to adults and children. (That would prove a challenge for the designers: The clients' tastes leaned towards luxurious textiles and antique furniture, and the proportions of the rooms were inherently stately.)

The bathrooms were largely designed with Carrara marble, porcelain and glass. Glamour was added to the master bath with antique light fixtures and furniture like this Billy Baldwin-designed slipper chair.

A moody Ed Ruscha painting gives an edge to this well-appointed living room while complementing its equally moody color scheme.

DESIGNER TIPS

**Update with Respect:** When rebuilding an antique home, don't be a slave to the original architecture. Respect certain aspects of the home's design, but update other components to create more interesting and contemporary rooms. It's a delicate balance, but if done right, you'll end up with a new classic.

**Plaster If You Can:** If there's room in your budget, consider plaster for the walls and moldings. Common until World War II (when sheet rock was discovered to be a faster, easier solution), plaster walls still lend a room old world appeal.

**Play with Shape and Forms:** Nahem says that large, imposing rooms can seem too "important" and off-putting, so he chooses furniture and accessories in a variety of shapes and forms, which distract the eye and bring the room down to size.

**Keep it in Proportion:** Tall ceilings require a balance between crown and base moldings, while paneling helps add dimensions to walls.

## Plaster's Old World Charm

Since the clients and designers were happy with the layout and size of the original rooms, including the placement of the kitchen and bathrooms, Fox and Nahem kept the basic structure intact. But that was about all they kept. "We had to completely gut the place and bring it down to the studs," says Nahem.

When they rebuilt the walls, Nahem and Fox decided to use plaster instead of sheetrock to give the space a worldly, lived-in feel. "If you can afford plaster, it's worth it," Nahem explains. "The French plaster we used looks like a fresco. There is such depth and beauty to it. The best faux painter couldn't duplicate its effect on sheetrock walls."

The designers then turned their attention to the home's other architectural details, including its moldings, doors, tiles and plumbing fixtures. Fox and Nahem also chose to have the new moldings made from plaster. "The original house had plaster moldings," Nahem says. "We decided to use plaster as well since it is hard to get big, beefy moldings from wood. We also used large moldings that would be in proportion with the rooms' tall ceilings." The crown moldings are around sixteen inches tall, while the base moldings measure about a foot.

## Retro Diner Design

While they rebuilt the architectural details, the firm also designed the kitchen and bathrooms. The kitchen's décor was somewhat inspired by classic 1950s diners, which often had exteriors (and sometimes interior) elements rounded off and clad in stainless steel. To create the effect of a diner—albeit a ritzy one—Fox and Nahem installed a custom-designed brown leather banquette, lined chairs up at a counter and used a row of vintage French stainless-steel cabinets,

This 19th-century American mantel, made from statuary marble, is paired with a circa-1900 Venetian mirror. The 7' by 14' mirror helps bridge the large gap between the mantel and the 14' ceiling, while a beefy, plaster base molding, helps bring the room down to human scale.

previously housed in a law office, as additional storage.

"The banquette can be a hard sell to clients, but we have used two so far and both families were really happy with them," says Nahem. "The novelty of having one in a home and their associations with an old-time diner make them appealing. They are comfortable and the family members gravitate towards them."

An intriguing combination of St. Charles cabinetry and freestanding 1920s cabinets lends the room a retro look while doing away with the monotony of built-in pieces. To complement the vintage design scheme, Fox and Nahem lined the cabinets along a wall that they had stripped down to its original texture-rich brick. "We didn't want this kitchen, like so many high-end kitchens today, to look like a cabinet showroom," says Nahem.

Two metal and glass light fixtures were all that was needed to finish the room. The copper-and-cut glass lantern over the banquette is French, from the 1940s. The one over the island, made from metal and seeded glass, is early 20th-century American. "We felt the light fixture above the island was most in keeping with the style of the original home," says Nahem.

## Adding Glamour

The living and dining rooms truly exemplify the glamour the clients desired. This effect is partly due to a selection of vintage fabrics sold through Manhattan's Cora Ginsburg, a purveyor of antique textiles. These high-end antiques, which include early 19th-century cut-laced velvet, add considerable warmth and style to the rooms they're in.

They also blend well with the living room's muted color scheme, which ranges from blue to gray to lavender. To subtly accent the subdued colors, which change with the natural light, the designers chose monochromatic silk drapes that gently puddle on to the floor. The upholstered pieces (some designed by Fox-Nahem) were then paired with wrought-iron and gilded-base tables, making the combined effect a delightful contrast between straight and curved forms. As a finishing touch, the Ed Ruscha painting over the sofa adds a reflective

The formal dining room's unusual wing chairs were styled after a pair of Italian chairs from the 1950s. They resemble classic forms, but their shape and rich upholstery give them a contemporary feel.

Nahem team wanted to preserve the stairs' original balustrade—a signature White design—because it was one of the few details still intact from the original townhouse.

## DESIGNER TIPS

**Aging Through Decorative Selections:** Although they can be very expensive, vintage fabrics lend a room a sense of age and authority. One cost-effective alternative is to buy new textiles based on antique patterns. Unusual antiques and vintage light fixtures will also do the trick, but make sure to choose pieces that stand out in a room.

**Glamorous and Feminine are Synonymous:** If you want your rooms to look glam, choose curvaceous upholstered, wood and iron furniture. Velvet, chenille and silks can look very feminine in the right setting. And stick with soothing, cool color schemes such as lavender, gray and pale blue.

**Think Outside the Box:** Instead of pairing a table with chairs, combine a dining table with a banquette. It works in both formal and informal spaces. Upholster it in leather for the kitchen and in velvet for a formal dining room.

**Blend Old and New:** Juxtapose antique and modern for exciting visual interest. For example, in a room with traditional paneling and moldings, hang contemporary art.

character to the room.

The dining room is one of the most dramatic areas in the home. While they would need to restore about 70 percent of it, the designers kept White's original oak paneling. The clients didn't want a stiff, formal dining room, so the restored paneling was mated with eclectic design elements to retain a comfortable, casual air.

While a brilliant, 300-year-old Venetian glass chandelier does contribute a sense of fomality to the space, the rest of the furnishings help soften the room's feel. The wing chairs were styled after two Italian pieces from the 1950s, which the firm found at Manhattan's Donzella, a retailer of 20th-century vintage furniture. And the large oak dining table, which seats 16, was custom-designed by Fox-Nahem. A large silk window panel and paintings from the clients' striking art collection complete the effect.

"There is an interesting balance at work in the dining room," says Nahem. "The paneling and chandelier suggest formality but the artwork, side table, dining chairs and window treatment offset the formal aspects, creating an exciting juxtaposition."

In this home, Fox-Nahem proves that even when reworking historic spaces, it's possible to blend old and new in a fresh way. In fact, by avoiding a painstaking line-by-line restoration, the designers were able to add contemporary interest to the house. And they did so without sacrificing period authenticity, retaining enough historic details to draw out the home's former glory while making it fashionable enough for modern lifestyles.

The den is both warm and inviting, thanks to its carefully-chosen textiles, animal skins and wood furniture. The dark tone of the built-in mahogany bookcase and moldings brings the walls in and makes the whole space feel intimate.

# ANTIQUES

1.

2.

3.

**KENTSHIRE GALLERIES** 1, 2, 3, 4
Over the last sixty-five years, Kentshire Galleries has developed a reputation as one of the premium sources for English antique furniture and accessories in the country. Run now by two brother-in-laws, Frederic Imberman and Robert Israel, the company has inventory dating from the late 17th century up through the 19th century. The gallery is large by New York standards—there are eight showroom floors designed as period room settings. Additionally, hundreds of objects can be seen on its website. Although prices aren't listed, a color-coded system gives a ballpark range from several thousand dollars to over fifty thousand; some prices go as high as several hundred thousand for items listed online. Price quotes can be obtained by email or a call to the showroom. Also, for those not well schooled in the history of interior design, the website lists a glossary of terms and information about famous cabinetmakers and the historical period in which they worked. Retail. **Call 212-673-6644 or visit www.kentshire.com.**

**INGRAO GALLERY**
In a historic townhouse on Manhattan's Upper East side, interior designer Anthony Ingrao has created a unique gallery setting. English antiques, silhouetted against a sleek contemporary backdrop, set a tone similar to the interior design popular with some of Ingrao's younger clients, who prefer loft-like interior architectural shells decorated with antiques. The gallery opened in 2002 and in the two years since, it has become an invaluable source for high-end decorators. In addition to English pieces, Ingrao carries antiques from Northern Europe and Russia among others, as well as contemporary paintings. Prices range from $20,000 to over $2 million. (To learn more about Ingrao's designs, see Chapter 7, *Georgian Redefined.*) To the Trade. **Call 212-472-5400.**

**HOWARD KAPLAN ANTIQUES**
A Parsons graduate, Howard Kaplan started in the antiques business 30 years ago after working as an interior designer. His 12,000 square-foot store, located in lower Manhattan, specializes in French and English 18th- and 19th-century antiques. The antiques range from country to formal, and include bath-related and salvaged architectural goods. The store also sells a wide variety of reproductions, from furniture to humorous French enamel signs. A sampling of antiques and most reproductions can be viewed on the

store's website. To learn more about this source, see the plumbing and architectural salvage sections. Retail. **Call 212-674-1000 or visit www.howardkaplanantiques.com.**

### COCONUT COMPANY

Former art dealer Constantin Von Haeften founded Manhattan's Coconut Company in 1995, selling largely Dutch Indonesian Colonial furniture. His inventory has become more eclectic since and today includes a wider variety of 19th- and 20th-century European, as well as American, furniture and Asian accessories. Designers compliment him for his unusual, even eccentric, choices. Retail. **Call 212-539-1940.**

### O'SULLIVAN ANTIQUES

Founded in 1992 in Ireland and established in New York in 1996, O'Sullivan Antiques deals in fine Georgian, Victorian and Edwardian furniture, largely from the green isle. Owned by Dublin-born Chantal O'Sullivan, who has worked in the antique business for over 20 years, it is the source designers go to for Irish antiques, which are known for their craftsmanship, durability and whimsy. The O'Sullivan Antiques website showcases a large selection of the store's items, including furniture, gilt mirrors, paintings, garden furniture, chimney pieces and objets d'art. Retail. **Call 212-260-8985 or visit www.osullivanantiques.com.**

### JOURDAN ANTIQUES

Founded by Mady Jourdan nearly twenty years ago, Jourdan Antiques carries a wide array of French furniture dating back to the 18th century. Objects range widely, from a circa 1800 formal French mahogany Directoire writing desk, to a 1930s engraved mirrored console. The 20th-century selection includes furniture from notable designers, including Emile Jacques Ruhlmann and Henri Jansen. In addition to antiques, Jourdan carries a line of contemporary furniture designed by her daughter Marie Guerin. **Call 212-674-4470 or visit www.jourdanantiques.com.**

### LAFAYETTE ANTIQUES AT THE WAREHOUSE

Lafayette Antiques at the Warehouse is located in an early 20th-century, 20,000-square-foot converted warehouse that takes up one city block in East Harlem. Within its walls are the collections of 50 international dealers who sell antiques in room settings, including Italian, African, Asian, English, French

### COMPANY IN FOCUS: ARTFACT

The Artfact website is an invaluable source for antiques, with a database of over 100 auction houses, ranging from internationally known houses like Christie's and Sotheby's, to prominent U.S. regional shops, including Boston's Skinner and Detroit's DuMouchelles. On Artfact's website, you can review unabridged auction catalogs and search for specific items, such as Tiffany lamps or Anglo-Raj armoires. Once you've found the antiques you want, you can attend the auctions or contact the auction houses directly to place a bid. Additionally, for a nominal daily rate or yearly professional fee, you can search Artfact's database of over 5 million auction results. Knowing the prices that specific antiques sold for in the past serves as a useful comparison when you're planning a purchase. With this auction tool, Artfact helps its customers make more confident purchases. Artfact was founded six years ago by Stephen Abt, a computer scientist and son of antique dealers. Abt had a vision for a single resource that would unite the complex and fragmented antiques and art market, making it more accessible to all. The company plans to eventually become an intermediary, so that customers can purchase antiques directly through the website.
**Visit www.artfact.com**.

4.

and American, all dating back to the 18th century. Parking is free and on-site. **Call 212-772-8400 or visit www.lafayetteantiques.com.**

1.

**FAIR TRADE** 1

For nearly twenty years, Bruce and Deborah Phillips of Fair Trade have been specializing in 19th-century Anglo-Raj and British Colonial antiques, including furniture, lighting and salvaged architectural pieces. The styles, which were built for ease of travel, are known for their exotic dark woods and exceptional craftsmanship. Most pieces were hand carved by English and Indian craftsmen for English officers during the occupation of India, or for Indian gentry. These styles have a strong English influence, though pieces produced in India tend to have more of an Asian sensibility. Fair Trade is located in Shelburne, MA and sells largely to the trade, but offers its goods to the public by appointment or when participating in antique shows in the New York and Connecticut area. See the antiques and show schedules on their website. Fair Trade will also search for requested antiques. **Call 866-337-8513 or visit www.fairtradeantiques.com.**

2.

**MAISON GERARD** 2, 3

Maison Gerard sells fine French and American art deco furniture and *objets d' art*, specializing in pieces from the 1920s to 1940s. The 4,000-square-foot, two-story antique store opened in Manhattan in the early 1970s and is owned by Gerard Widdershoven (the founder) and Denoist F. Drut. It frequently hosts furniture designer shows dedicated to individual furniture makers, such as LeLeu and Ruhlmann. In addition to furniture, Maison Gerard sells an extensive collection of Danish decorative arts, including ceramics and metals. **Call 212-674 7611 or visit www.maisongerard.com.**

3.

**BROADWAY ANTIQUE MARKET**

Considered by many designers as the best source for vintage items from the 1930s through the 1950s, Chicago's Broadway Antique Market, co-owned by Danny Alias and Jeff Nelson, offers goods from 70 different dealers in a 20,000-square-foot space. A selection of its goods is available for sale at its website. Products vary greatly, from an 1885 Victorian aesthetic movement Bon Bon Tray, to a 1930s Art Deco chrome and vinyl club chair. It's the source many film and TV prop designers shop for campy, retro items. **Call 773-743-5444 or visit www.bamchicago.com.**

**J. TRIBBLE ANTIQUES** 4

Located in Atlanta, J. Tribble Antiques is known for its Art Deco and Biedermeier antique furniture and its custom reproductions, including a diverse line of cabinets that can be used as sink bases. The owners, John Tribble, who studied antiques at Sotheby's, and Rebecca Fincher, who is an interior designer, founded the company in 1997. Products can be viewed on the website. Retail. **Call 888-652-6116 or visit www.jtribbleantiques.com.**

4.

**PAGODA RED** 5, 6

Chicago's Pagoda Red was founded seven years ago by Betsy Nathan. It has become a leading resource for Chinese furniture and accessories dating back to the 18th century. In her 20s, Nathan had moved to Beijing to learn Mandarin and lived in an area where antiques were sold. Once exposed to the furniture trade, she decided to return to the U.S. and become a dealer. Pagoda Red is known for its pieces from the Northern Province of Shanxi, Deco blackwood furniture from Shanghai and architectural artifacts. A large selection of furniture is available for viewing online. Retail. **Call 773-235-1188 or visit www.pagodared.com.**

5.

6.

**ANTIQUES CENTERS**

Forty-five minutes north of New York City, there are a series of warehouses that have been converted into antique centers. Located within minutes of each other, they house hundreds of individual antique booths, carrying tens of thousands of goods. Collectively, the antique centers carry a wide array of antique styles and a range of goods from furniture to accessories to fine art. Designers, including Jack Fhillips, say visiting the warehouses is well worth the trip, citing the variety, quality and prices. Retail.

**Hiden Galleries:** Call 203-323-9090 or visit www.hiden-galleries-antiques.com.

**The Antique & Artisan Center:** Call 203-327-6022 or visit www.stamfordantiquescenter.com.

**Harbor View Center for Antiques:** Call 203-325-8070 or visit www.harborviewantiques.net.

**Shippan Center for Arts & Antiques:** 203-353-0222 or visit www.shippancenter.com.

**Debbie's Stamford Antiques Center:** Call 888-329-3546.

# CHAPTER 3

# REVIVAL CHIC

Interior designer Elissa Cullman and architect Ira Grandberg design historically-inspired homes for contemporary lifestyles. Whether they're modeled after English Tudors or early American farmhouses, their designs charmingly resemble the originals, though the team takes pains to make sure the layout and interiors still cater to the needs of today's families. Their secret: Incorporating striking artwork and antiques, and avoiding formulaic architectural plans and artificial design details.

The duo is especially well-matched: In the two homes featured here, Cullman chose most of the artwork, furniture, fabric and other interiors elements, while Grandberg designed the architecture and the majority of the interior structural details.

## The Art of the Interior Designer

Elissa Cullman, of Manhattan-based Cullman & Kravis, is probably best known for the folk art she uses in her home designs. (Although her work is far more diverse, it is generally the folk art designs that makes its way onto the pages of interiors magazines.) The former guest curator of The Museum of American Folk Art and co-author of a book on the depiction of children in folk art, titled *Small Folk: A Celebration of Childhood in America*, Cullman has a love for this primitive art form, and it is often a key element in the rooms she designs.

When Cullman and her (late) partner Heidi Kravis first started practicing interior design in the 1980s, folk art wasn't widely collected by the type of people who hired high-end designers. "There was no canon to decorating with folk art, which allowed me to be more creative with it," says Cullman. "It is an incredibly versatile art form. The pieces' simplicity makes them abstract and modern, similar to pop art."

**Opposite:** Grandberg likens the design of this Tudor-style home to a series of linked garden sheds. The clients wanted its interior spaces to be intimate and oriented towards its English-inspired landscaping. Although the home is large and expansive, nearly all the rooms have easy access to the outdoors.

This double-height foyer, similar to an English great hall, boasts a handsome antique mantel and rich wooden beams. A sense of proportion in its furnishings, accessories and light fixtures makes the space feel less intimidating, while the large hanging lantern brings the eye down and, by extension, your perception of the room's size.

**Incorporate a Range of Periods:** Although you want your rooms to look antique, choosing everything from one design period will make your home look like a museum. When selecting furnishings, look for relationships that aren't strictly historical. Instead, find a variety of pieces that you love and use them together. A fine balance between historical accuracy and originality will add sophistication and character to your rooms.

**Adapt Antiques:** Use an armoire that stored clothing in the 19th century as a wine or TV cabinet today. Use an old-fashioned silver chest as a coffee table. Don't be afraid to use your antiques—just make sure you care for them properly.

**Make it Comfortable:** A home should be as welcoming and comfortable as it is pretty. It should be designed in a way that makes your guests feel relaxed. Remember: Homes are for enjoying family, friends and life.

**Enrich Spaces with Antiques and Art:** By combining fine art and antiques with architectural elements of historic periods you will create rooms with character, rhythm and exciting juxtapositions of old and new. Antiques and fine art add an enriching layer of beauty and meaning to every interior.

**Make Space for Your Hobbies:** Incorporate your personality into the design of your home by acknowledging your hobbies and passions. One of Cullman's most challenging assignments was to highlight a client's obsession with snakes in the décor of her entry foyer. The solution: a custom stencil pattern that included "friendly-looking" snakes and the client's initials.

**Remember the Details:** Add character to your spaces by using salvaged architectural elements, including mantels, reclaimed wood and stone, and old bathroom fixtures. If suitable old pieces can't be found, have them custom-made by a local artist in the spirit of the antique equivalent, using details that are respectful of the period. The more background you give the artisan, the better the final product will be.

The once-utilitarian pieces—weathervanes, hooked rugs, ceramic vessels—add character to new rooms. "Folk art brings refinement and elegance to gigantic, new homes that are lacking a soul," Cullman explains. "It references a nostalgic time in our country's history."

Done well, folk art infuses rich surroundings with charm and whimsy. One of Cullman's many talents is the way she incorporates it into sophisticated interiors. "At my firm, we love to work in a style that we call 'opposites attract,'" the designer says. "We once mixed a client's folk art collection from her country house with the Biedermeier furniture in her Fifth Avenue penthouse. The folk art made the furniture look less slick and urban, and the Biedermeier made the folk art look more sophisticated. Discovering a shared aesthetic between the elegant and the humble can create thoughtful harmony throughout a space."

In addition to folk art, Cullman favors American paintings, photographs and drawings from the 19th and 20th centuries. "I use artwork to demonstrate the personalities of the people who live in the homes we design," Cullman says. "I take a thematic approach and develop a narrative thread. There has to be cohesion to the artwork for it to be successful as a design element."

Cullman creates collections that look like they have evolved over the years, which enriches the newly-constructed rooms they adorn. If budget is a concern, she introduces her clients to undiscoverd artists and photographers, from whose

This room exemplifies the sophisticated textures and patterns at play in Cullman's work. The antique "bamboo-turned" wooden vanity is nicely paired with a wicker-and-wood chair, while plaid draperies are counterbalanced by floral cushions.

"**Folk art** *adds refinement and elegance to gigantic, new homes that are lacking* **a soul.** *"It gives a reference to a* **nostalgic** *period of our country's history."*

Simple unadorned portraits, a carved wooden sculpture and an antique, weathered clock bring character to a new room.

work they can build a more affordable collection. To keep things interesting, she incorporates more than one style and period. "There has to be an overall point of view, but that doesn't mean all the artwork has to come from one artist or be in one style," Cullman says.

The designer relies on antiques to give the rooms a sense of history. "At my firm, we love to use antiques because of their beauty and rarity, and the layers of meaning and interest they add to rooms by their connection to the past," she explains. "Yet we never allow the collections to dominate or to dictate lifeless, museum-like rooms. Rather, they should enliven, enrich and enhance the atmosphere of the homes."

Again, there is a narrative element to the antiques she chooses for each home. "We might design one with all country furniture, but include pieces from France, England, America and Africa," Cullman says. "Or use dark, turned wood or carved wood from different areas and periods. The pieces can be different if they share the same connection."

Cullman's rooms are made complete by her use of complex color schemes, comfortably upholstered furniture, decorative accessories, texture-rich carpeting, and area rugs and textiles.

## The Architect's Style

Ira Grandberg, based in Mount Kisco, N.Y., is considered the man to got to when you want a new home that looks truly antique. Many architects and developers don't take the time to properly reinterpret historical styles, but Grandberg creates authentic, aesthetically pleasing homes with great flourish. In practice for 25 years, he specializes in high-end estate homes.

"None of our projects start out with a formulaic plan, unlike many of the Georgian-style homes being built today,"

**Opposite:** This well-appointed dining room showcases antiques, with the exception of an attractive and updated ceiling grid that echoes the wall paneling. The brass chandelier has three tiers, which bring the eye down and make the room feel more intimate.

Grandberg says. "People feel comfortable with panels, moldings, and other textural materials from the 18th-century Georgian period, but the challenge is to use these materials creatively as an integral part of the space, and not merely as window dressing. Homes that look like stage sets have no soul or sense of history to them."

When reinterpreting a historic architectural style, Grandberg focuses on the details, intent on making sure his homes look authentic. "All the details are very important," he says. "Architects are trained to pay attention to them.

Developers typically don't have that training, so they don't understand what makes a home work. The more honest the architecture is, the better the home and the more true to the style it looks."

## The Newly Old Homes

Cullman and Grandberg updated the two historic homes featured here to suit the contemporary needs of their owners. While honoring the scale of the dwellings themselves, they altered the size of their rooms, their traditional layouts and the number and size of their windows. The addition of modern appliances and technologies, and the lightening up of their interior color schemes gave these historical homes a modern edge without compromising their integrity or style.

The first home was styled after England's late 19th-century Tudor-style Cotswold cottages. Although the clients wanted a large home, they asked that its interior scale be similar to a garden shed, and that many of its rooms have direct access to the outdoors. So instead of replacing the three existing 1890s Tudor-style buildings on the property, which were fairly dilapidated, Grandberg linked and structurally rehabilitated them, creating a home that is expansive yet cozy. The combined structure is 22,000 square feet, but its rooms feel intimate, largely because of their scale. Its stone foundation gives the home the impression of naturally growing out of the earth, as many original Tudors seem to do.

Grandberg says his firm used a post-and-beam infrastructure to link the buildings, create open, informal spaces and establish an architectural scale that would be carried throughout the house, both in the interior and exterior. Expert craftsmen constructed the authentic half-timber exterior. "The real Tudor homes were special because of their construction techniques," explains Grandberg. "In order to properly build a Tudor today, you must use the same building techniques that were used to build the originals. People get tired of superficial details very quickly."

The interior of the house is also inspired by traditional English design. There are exposed posts and beams, hand-carved stone fireplaces, rough-hewn wall surfaces and stone and wooden floors. Much of the interior wood was limed to make it look lighter than the original Tudor homes' dark paneling and beams. The color scheme is dominated by beige and green.

"It's a happy Tudor," Cullman reflects. "I think of it as an American interpretation of the English vernacular. The

This unexpected collection of colored glassware, on display in a secondary entranceway, imparts the spirit of the home's Colonial-inspired interior design.

interiors are lighter in color and more lighthearted in design. The paneling is not darkly stained, there are lots of windows and the furniture is not heavy. It is a very uplifting home."

The second home featured was originally built in 1800, with several Colonial-style additions made later that century. Its new owners wanted to more than double the home's size—to make room for their children's growing families—but they didn't want to lose its early American charm.

Grandberg decided to work around the original scale of the house, reorganizing the existing layout and adding more rooms for more space. He created new sight lines throughout the home that offered improved views of the landscape and artwork, while also increasing the amount of light that

Contemporary framed photography and antique furnishings, combined with folk art accessories and a chandelier, create positive tension in this informal dining area. A ceiling of wooden planks makes an old-fashioned impression, suggesting that it was built before the advent of gypsum board.

DESIGNER TIPS

**Be Creative with Paint:** Monchromatic walls are not typical of historical homes. Work with artists to find glazes, stencils and murals that evoke the past. If you do stick to one color, use oil-based paint, which oxidizes and ages well.

**Make It Antique:** Build antique architectural details into rooms instead of applying them as surface decoration. Copy the floors, wall treatments, molding and masonry of historic homes. New homes fail to look antique when veneers such as stone are applied.

**Consider Sight Lines:** Think of sight lines when you lay out your floor plan. Proper sight lines create vistas and bring in natural light.

**Add Light:** Although light-filled, airy rooms were not common in historic houses, they are desirable today. Update Tudor and Colonial homes by making the rooms and windows larger and choosing a lighter stain for flooring, paneling and other natural wooden elements.

**Create a Sense of Scale:** Although developers make their homes "opulent" with a lot of double-height spaces, this often looks awkward in historically styled homes, as many of the original versions didn't have tall ceilings. To properly integrate rooms of this scale into a traditional dwelling, use architectural details like trim, molding and flooring in larger rooms and add strong-looking ceiling beams or unusual ceilings such as tin or tray styling to bring the scale down.

penetrates the home. "The house was typically Colonial with dark, cavernous rooms and low ceilings," Grandberg says. "We wanted to keep the original home's scale but create larger, lighter rooms with better views."

The home retains its Colonial spirit largely because the low ceiling heights are carried throughout. Grandberg's use of traditionally paned windows, antique moldings and salvaged, wide oaken floorboards, also contribute to its authentic feel.

"The original Colonial homes were dark and had narrow rooms," explains Cullman. "In those homes, you expected to look in the corner and see a Puritan reading the Bible. This home is open, warm, cheerful and modern."

The interior of the home is decorated in an upscale Colonial farmhouse style. Cullman was asked to expand the clients' collection of American and English antiques and blend them with their existing photography collection, which featured both vintage and contemporary images. An expert at using art collections in interior design, Cullman skillfully hung the photography alone or in groupings throughout the home. The framed photos give this Colonial-style dwelling a refreshing and rarely seen edge, adding a strong theatrical counterpoint to the home's antiques and folk art.

With their mix of the modern and traditional, the design team had given these new spaces happy, old souls.

**Above:** The color palette of this paneled pine library is dominated by the wood's rich, honeyed tone. (Cullman brought out this the color by having the wood hand-rubbed and waxed.) The combination of accessories in the shelves—books, folk art and vintage ceramics—look as if they naturally evolved over time.

**Above:** Honey-toned woodwork unites this room with adjoining areas, while creating a character-rich space for the owner's collection of English and American antiques and accessories.

In one of the Colonial home's few rooms with tall ceiling heights, Grandberg installed a tray ceiling. A continuous shelf was also introduced to bring the eye down and create the perception that the room is the same scale as the rest of the home. The shelf is stocked with 19th-century French ceramic pitchers and has a Sturbridge Village-inspired stencil running the length of it. Such details help distract it from the room's height.

# RESTORED & HAND-PAINTED FURNITURE

*Interior designers often turn to a select group of top antique restorers for their clients' most precious items. The two Manhattan-based specialists profiled in this chapter are among the best in the country, so let their profiles and tips guide your search for skilled workmen. For further information on how to find local reputable refinishers, see the section on trade tips. The other sources in this chapter are manufacturers of fine hand-painted furniture sold through showrooms across the U.S. or over the internet.*

1.

2.

**ARTISANS: ELI RIOS, ECR ANTIQUE CONSERVATION AND RESTORATION** 1

If you were to ask a Manhattan museum or auction house to recommend a furniture restorer, you'd likely be sent to Eli Rios of ECR Antique Conservation and Restoration. Rios began his training at the age of 12, working alongside an uncle who ran a cabinetmaking shop. By 1980, he was working in Sotheby's restoration department, where he was promoted to senior restorer within four years. In 1987, Rios opened his own workshop; today, he has a 10,000-square-foot space in Manhattan's Chelsea neighborhood. The restorer says his craft requires him to be equal parts artist, architectural historian, detective and alchemist. "I'm Colombo," he jokes. "At the Smithsonian, I studied the chemistry of historic materials, so I know how to restore an item to its original finish and spot fakes."

3.

Rios has since developed his own line of stains, shellacs and related restoration products, which are highly popular with both professionals and DIY types. The wood stains are created from walnut crystals, while the organic furniture shellac is made from insects' resin. (Polyurethane, he says, should only be used on floors.) "The point of restoration is to make furniture look as if nothing was done to it," Rios says. "I like to restore it in the same way that it was first made—to carve as the original carver did, using mostly antique hand tools and natural products." When not working on antiques, Rios makes "exact copies" of vintage items and teaches other students about his restoration techniques. Retail. **Call 866-643-0388 or visit www.ecrios.com.**

4.

**ARTISANS: JOSEPH BIUNNO** 2

Joseph Biunno's antique restoration business really began in the early 20th century, when his grandfather left Naples to open up shop in Manhattan. A professional restorer, the elder Biunno had

5.

extremely high standards, inspiring (two) successive generations to follow his lead. In 1950, Joseph's father took over the business and became known for his high-quality work, with a clientele that included legendary designers Albert Hadley, Dorothy Draper and Billy Baldwin. In the 1970s, young Joseph expanded the firm's size and services, also adding to its prestigious list of customers. Restoration work occasionally requires antique hand tools, and so is often done by trained craftsmen—many of whom learn their trade in Eastern Europe. At Biunno's 10,000-square-foot loft in Manhattan's flower district, carvers, turners, guilders, cabinetmakers, finishers and metalworkers combine forces to expertly restore pieces. No detail is left unattended when Biunno refinishes and repairs an antique: He even duplicates the hardware needed to replace missing locks and keys. The shop also offers high-end antique reproductions, window treatments and other hardware; owner Biunno says the expert craftsmen and quick turnaround keep customers coming back. For more information, see the sections on window treatments and hardware. Retail. **Call 212-629-5630 or visit www.antiquefurnitureusa.com.**

**COUNTRY SWEDISH** 3

In the mid-1980s, Richard and Estelle deJounge owned an antiques store in Westport, CT that specialized in the Swedish Gustavian furniture they grew up with. Created during the reign of Sweden's King Gustav III, these pieces are a blend of classic Italian, French and English styles from the 17th and 18th centuries painted or glazed in muted hues. The Swedish couple noted a lack of available Gustavian antiques and began making reproductions which are handcrafted and hand-painted in Scandinavia. The deJounges partnered with compatriot Cecilia Hirshorn in 2003 and their business currently encompasses a Country Swedish store, four showrooms, a catalog and a website, and also offers a range of wallpaper, accessories, fabrics and rugs. To the Trade. **Call 212-838-1976 or visit www.countryswedish.com.**

**JULIA GRAY** 4

For nearly 20 years, former interior designer Julia Gray has been selling high quality, hand-painted furniture inspired by the 18th-century antiques she acquires on trips to Europe. There are about 150 pieces in her line, most made from birch and all painted by artisans in her workshop. But Gray also offers custom-painting services, which many designers use, including Scott Salvator. She gets the most requests for chinoiserie styles and geometric patterns that feature cross-hatching and trellising. Julia Gray is available at seven showrooms in major design centers across the country, and can also be ordered by catalogue. For more information about this source, see the section on reproduction furniture. To the Trade. **Call 212-223-4454.**

**DECORATIVE CRAFTS** 5, 6

For over 75 years, family-run Decorative Crafts has been importing handmade goods from Italy, including an extensive line of hand-detailed, historically inspired furniture. Some of its furniture is elaborately painted, such as a 17th-century Italian-style credenza with antique-looking fruit and florals. Other pieces simply have colorful accents, like the company's 18th-century French-style light pickled bombé chest, highlighted in gold leaf. Based in Greenwich, CT, Decorative Crafts has six showrooms in major US cities; free catalogs are available through its website. For more on this source, see the section on accessories. To the Trade or retail through Izolli. (See trade tips section for Izolli contact info.) **Call 800-431-4455 or visit www.decorativecrafts.com.**

6.

**AUFFRAY & CO.** 7

At the end of the 19th century, master cabinetmaker Frederic Auffray opened his first store in Paris. In 1941, his son Joachim made his way to the United States, where he introduced the family business to Manhattan. Today, this esteemed American shop carries furniture spanning 150+ years of French design, from the grand baroque Louis XIV period to the military-inspired Directoire era. All of the pieces are crafted and finished in Auffray & Co.'s Manhattan workshop; most are hand-painted and can be customized to meet your needs. For prices and information on how to order, see the company website or catalog, or check out the showrooms in New York and Boston. To the Trade. **Call 212-889-4646 or visit www.auffray.com.**

7.

# ARCHITECTURAL SALVAGE

*Adding architectural salvage to a home is no different than including antiques—it's a great way to bring old world feeling to a new space. Salvage prices differ widely, depending on provenance and availability, as well as the retailer's mark-up. Some pieces, including bath fittings and doors, are frequently less expensive than reproductions; others, such as stone fireplace mantels and stained-glass windows, can be very costly. Designers either love working with salvage or flat-out reject it: Finding and refurbishing the right piece involves far more work than just buying a reproduction. Yet those who use it say it's worth the effort. Local dealers may not have as wide a selection as you'd find on the Internet, but they come in handy when you're buying larger pieces (doors, mantels, bathtubs), as you avoid expensive shipping costs. To find dealers in your area, contact local demolition contractors or historical preservation societies. Online dealers may be able to send extra photos of items that interest you; be sure to inquire about shipping costs and return policies.*

*Salvaged pieces run the gamut from floorboards to keyhole escutcheons and fireplace mantels, and even vintage commodes and radiators are in high demand. Basically, any item used before 1950 to construct or decorate the framework of a building is now sold as salvage. The following architectural salvage retailers have websites that allow you to view their vintage and antique goods.*

**COMPANY IN FOCUS: OLDE GOOD THINGS**

Despite its humble beginnings, Olde Good Things has grown into one of the country's largest dealers of salvaged architecture. Things started inauspiciously in the late 1980s, when members of The Church of Bible Understanding began selling discarded and donated goods at local flea markets. Architectural relics soon proved very profitable, so in 1989, church members decided to open a salvage store in Brooklyn, NY. Today they have five locations—three in New York, one in California and an 85,000+-square-foot retail warehouse in Pennsylvania. (When profits are not fed back into the church, they go to fund charitable works in Haiti, where they support the operation of three orphanages.) The company carries everything from doors, doorknobs, hardware and mantels to decorative iron, stained glass and terra cotta pieces. One recent store visit unearthed an antique bronze doorknocker that had been rescued from a dismantled castle, a white marble wall fountain last seen on Wall Street and a copper Art Deco panel that once adorned a power company building. At its Pennsylvania warehouse, Olde Good Things also offers an abundance of lawn and garden salvage, including wrought-iron patio furniture. The company makes stops at antiques shows across the country; a schedule is listed on its website, as are prices and some products. Bartering is welcomed (see the "Make an Offer" icon on product pages). **Call 212-989-8401 or visit www.oldegoodthings.com.**

**THE DEMOLITION DEPOT**

In 2001, longtime architectural forager Evan Blum opened Manhattan's 20,000-square-foot Demolition Depot. Just the year before, his Irreplaceable Artifacts store had collapsed, taking with it a vast stockpile of goods. Demolition's got everything you'd ever want, from classic antiques to campy collectibles and one-of-a-kind treasures. A recent visit revealed a dismantled Louis XV-style paneled room, a vintage Magic Chef iron and enamel stove, and an Asian-inspired Broadway backdrop. Demolition's website lists most of the items for sale, without prices. Retail. **Call 212-860-1138 or visit www.demolitiondepot.com.**

**PIONEER MILLWORKS** 1, 2

Located in Farmington, NY, Pioneer Millworks sells flooring, timbers and millwork rescued from demolition sites. Recent acquisitions include early 20th-century Douglas Fir timbers removed from a renovated Canadian canal and rafters from a General Motors plant in New York. Pioneer also has a steady stream of wood from dismantled barns in the Northeast. The salvage company sells dozens of species and grades of wood through dealers across the country and in Canada. A catalog is available. See the section on floors for more information on this source. Retail and To the Trade. **Call 800-951-9663 or visit www.pioneermillworks.com.**

1.

2.

**CORNERSTONE**

Cornerstone is located in a charming 19th-century brick warehouse in Brooklyn, NY, where it sells items from dismantled European cathedrals and estates—including terra-cotta from demolished French châteaus and lumber from pre-war American and European buildings. The firm has become known for its reclaimed ceramics, stones and wood, but it also carries a wide range of salvage, including fireplace mantels, doors, bath fittings and accessories. Many Cornerstone products are imported from France, England, Africa and Asia; the company website does not list prices. Retail. **Call 718-855-2673 or visit www.cornerstonesalvage.com.**

**HOWARD KAPLAN ANTIQUES**

Howard Kaplan started his business 30 years ago, after attending the Parsons School of Design and working as an interior designer. These days, his 12,000-square-foot store, located in lower Manhattan, specializes in 18th- and 19th-century French bathroom furnishings, selling basics (bathtubs, commodes, sinks) as well as hardware and lighting. Standard items include antique wooden sink bases with Carrara marble countertops, classic claw-footed tubs and nickel-plated cup and soap holders. The store also sells bath-related reproductions, a sampling of which can be viewed on its website. See the sections on antiques for more information on this source. Retail. **Call 212-674-1000 or visit www.howardkaplanantiques.com.**

**ARCHITECTURAL ARTIFACTS**
Located in an 80,000-square-foot warehouse, Chicago's Architectural Artifacts was founded in 1987 by Stuart Grannen, a longtime dealer of antiquities. Grannen has filled his store with high-quality American and European architectural antiques, ranging from 19th-century marble mantels to 20th-century cast-iron griffin sconces and Frank Lloyd Wright leaded glass windows. A large portion of its inventory is displayed (and shown from various angles) on its sophisticated website. Retail. **Call 773-348-0622 or visit www.architecturalartifacts.com.**

1.

2.

**PARIS CERAMICS** 1, 2
Despite its name, Paris Ceramics is largely known for its premium-quality "rescued" stones, including antique terra cotta and centuries-old Jerusalem limestone. British founder Charlie Smallbone started the company in 1982, after discovering the beauty and appeal of reclaimed materials while running his own London-based custom kitchen firm, Smallbone of Devizes. In addition to finding unusual stones, his new business quarries its own and carries hand-painted decorative and glazed tiles, marble mosaics and cosmati patterns. Paris Ceramics has nine showrooms in the U.S. and one in England. See the section on floors for more information on this source. To the Trade. **Call 888-845-3487 or visit www.parisceramics.com.**

**FAIR TRADE** 3
For nearly 20 years, Bruce and Deborah Phillips of the Shelburne, MA-based Fair Trade have been specializing in 19th-century Anglo Raj and British colonial antiques, including salvaged architectural pieces retrieved from dismantled palaces and estates in India. Their stunning collection is highlighted by intricately carved, solid teak columns and ornate cast-iron balustrades. Sold largely to the industry, Fair Trade's products are shown to the public by appointment and can often be seen at New York- and Connecticut-area antiques shows. Products, prices and show schedules are available on the company website. See the sections on antiques for more information on this source. Retail. **Call 866-337-8513 or visit www.fairtradeantiques.com.**

**COMPANY IN FOCUS: ARCHITECTURALS.NET**
Architecturals.net is a subsidiary of Urban Development Corporation (UDC), a private company that has been rehabilitating vacant and dilapidated low-income housing in Philadelphia since 1996. To help sustain its business, UDC started to sell salvaged architectural items from the buildings it refurbished, a side project so successful that it spawned its own website, www.architecturals.net. Shoppers can now troll for salvage and antiques from the UDC's homes as well as from a broad array of international antique salvage dealers. Products range from 18th-century wooden fish-scale shingles to 19th-century hand-carved Spanish cedar doors and 20th-century wrought-iron balcony grates from France. Prices are listed, as are links to private dealers, whom shoppers can contact directly. The best part: Website proceeds help fight urban decay. Retail. **Call 800-658-5096 or visit www.architecturals.net.**

**UNITED HOUSE WRECKING**

Back in 1954, the Lodato family was hired to clear the way for Interstate 95 by demolishing homes in the New York tri-state area. The family quickly amassed a wealth of architectural cast-offs, and so opened United House Wrecking (UHW), a salvage and antiques dealership. Now located in a 35,000-square-foot space in Stamford, CT, UHW also sells accessories and lawn and garden décor, and has since broadened its inventory to include salvage and antiques from around the world. Designers praise UHW's wide variety and reasonable costs; product photos are available on the company website, though prices are not. Retail. **Call 203-348-5371 or visit www.unitedhousewrecking.com.**

**HISTORIC HOUSEPARTS**

Located in a 14,000-square-foot antique row house in Rochester, NY, Historic Houseparts sells architectural items salvaged from pre-1940s buildings. Among the treasures rescued from its demolished western New York sites are antique wooden medicine cabinets, intricate iron garden gates and cast-iron bin pulls. The company also carries a line of reproduction hardware, including push-button switches, bronze handle pulls and tin ceiling tiles. Its website offers a large selection of its goods, with prices; a catalog with reproductions and selected vintage items is available. Retail. **Call 888-558-2329 or visit www.historichouseparts.com.**

**OLD HOUSE PARTS**

Located in an enormous, 100-year-old barn in Maine, Old House Parts specializes in an eclectic array of items from the 18th to early 20th centuries. In addition to cast-iron doorknobs, stained-glass windows and claw-footed bathtubs, the company carries about 1,500 interior and exterior doors, dating back to the early 1700s, and leaded and beveled windows from as far back as the 1800s. Old House Parts can also construct character-rich sheds and playhouses from reclaimed lumber and antiques. For a look at products and prices, see the company website. Retail. **Call 207-985-1999 or visit www.oldhouseparts.com.**

3.

JACK PHILLIPS



# CHAPTER 4

# ANGLO-CARIBBEAN

If you're looking for traditional English style in a tropical setting, Jack Phillips should be at the top of your list. The interior designer is an Anglophile and antiquarian who just happens to have spent most of his life on or near the water. Combining his fondness for the beach with an in-depth knowledge of historical design, Phillips creates waterside homes that are one-of-a-kind pieces full of intriguing details, yet still seem carefree, crisp and breezy.

"Suitability, suitability, suitability—I can't stress it enough," Phillips says. "And location, location, location. The homes have to suit the location. If they are on the water, you can't try to compete with the view by overly decorating the rooms. You have to choose a color scheme that complements them and encourages the eye to move out towards the water. Waterside homes can be decorated with rich architectural details and antiques, but they have to be added in such a way that they enrich the spaces but don't take away from the main attraction."

Phillips, who has offices and a retail design store in Palm Beach, is basically an autodidact. Born in Cuba, he moved to the States as a young boy and was schooled in the Deep South, graduating from Georgia Southern University with a B.A. in Historic Preservation Design. Though he took a few design classes and worked for a designer shortly after graduation, he is largely self-taught.

"I received most of my education from interior design magazines," says Phillips. "I started reading them in my early teens. My first magazine subscription was to *House Beautiful*. My parents thought I was nuts and wanted me to be an attorney. But I loved color and

**Opposite:** This home's exterior is fashioned after 15th- and 16th-century Anglo-Caribbean dwellings, but with the open-ended loggias frequently seen in Palm Beach mansions. Built on pilings to avoid flood damage, the home has a massive porch, which is often used for outdoor entertaining.

Sea glass provided the inspiration for this vacation home's color scheme. Its pale, washed out colors are soothing, while allowing the home's main attraction, views of Bank's Channel, to take center stage.

In the informal dining room, an antique English mahogany table with satin wood inlay takes center stage. This magnificent piece is paired with Indonesian ebony side chairs and two wing chairs fashioned after the classic style, but modified for dining. White linen sheers add softness to the airy space, yet blend into the walls, where they do not distract from the impressive view.

DESIGNER TIPS

**Orient Your Home:** Waterfront vacation homes should look the part. All interior design should be oriented towards the view.

**Leave Delicate Antiques Behind:** Beach houses should be comfortable. Precious antiques generally do not belong here.

**Use Compatible Colors and Designs:** Chose complementary, not competing, color schemes. Avoid overdecorating. Water views are expansive, light and airy, and interiors that adjoin them should duplicate the effect.

**Stain Your Furniture with Dark Colors:** Dark furniture placed against light walls creates a silhouette effect that makes pieces look sculptural. Furniture in silhouette has a strong presence, so you'll need fewer pieces to make rooms appear full.

**Plan the Layout, then Shop:** When planning the design of a new home or room, start with the floor plan. Take into account your family's needs today and in the years to come. Then do what Phillips does and go fabric shopping. Let the complementary fabrics that appeal to you be your guide for your other design choices.

texture and furniture. I was so inspired—and still am today—by historical design. Towards the end of my parents' lives, they realized I would have made a rotten attorney."

## Vacation Home Design

Phillips' waterfront designs range from light, airy homes filled with eclectic antique furniture and bright colors to more serious-looking residences designed with British colonial pieces and muted color schemes. On the whole, the homes Phillips decorates are unpretentious and comfortable, with lots of vintage appeal.

The vacation home profiled in this chapter, located in the Wrightsville Beach section of North Carolina's South Harbor Island, was built after 1996's Hurricane Fran demolished the nearly 70 year-old cottage previously on the site. Wilmington-based architect Michael Ross Kersting designed the new home as a "flood-zone structure," built on pilings.

Enlisted from the beginning, Phillips helped the owners settle on the architectural style of their new dwelling, which was modeled after the Anglo-Caribbean homes first seen in the tropics in the 1600s. Those antique homes were known for their concrete structure, solid massing and hipped roofs. They blended traditional Caribbean style with English architecture and interior design.

## Design Approach

The clients' 6,000 square-foot home presented several challanges, not the least of which was how to create a floor plan that would allow the space to "grow" with its occupants. "A good plan will meet clients' current needs for space and storage yet suit them as they age and become less active," Phillips says. "Some new homes are so huge that it seems as if the master suite and its bathroom are in

The size and location of this Federal-style secretary helps establish it as a strong presence in the room. It creates a striking silhouette, adds a period note and moderates the effect of a 14-foot ceiling.

different wings, while the kitchen is so far away, it might as well be in a different house. Extremely large rooms in equally large homes become a problem as people grow older."

Once he had developed a strong floor plan, Phillips moved on to fabric selection. "The fabrics clients respond to will dictate the entire interior design," he explains. "If my clients are drawn to bright blue and white cotton fabrics that have images of florals and seashells, they will want their home to be bright, casual, fun and oriented toward the beach. If they choose neutral tones with lots of texture, they'll want a home that is more serious—maybe styled after some of the great British colonial homes. Fabric selection really sets the tone for a house."

The master bedroom looks comfortably old-fashioned, thanks to its antiques, ruffled bedskirt and canopy, floral upholstery fabric and vintage botanical prints. The bed, a reproduction, reaches towards the 12-foot ceiling, tempering its height.

"The homes have to **suit** the **location.** If they are on the **water**, you can't try to **compete** with the view by **overly decorating** the rooms."

Phillips updated this Victorian chair by upholstering it in raffia, a textile created from woven palm leaves that perfectly suits a waterfront home. The early 20th-century nautical advertisement placed by the bed adds an amusing vintage touch to the room.

In this case, Phillips' clients were drawn to fabrics that had an old-fashioned quality to them and came in a range of muted sea-glass colors. "I could tell by their fabric selection that they wanted an island-y home, but one with a historical Southern reference," the designer says. "The soft, mellow colors of sea glass-celadon, pale yellows and blues and cottony whites—are what you commonly see in older Southern houses. They work here because they complement the view and have a nostalgic appeal."

Phillips' homes are always filled with unique pieces. To add further historical references, he stocked the South Harbor home with English antiques and high-quality reproductions from the Regency, Jacobean, Georgian and Edwardian eras of the 17th and 18th centuries. The dark, wooden furniture chosen for the home was finely crafted, often with turned legs and posts.

"Antiques make me tick," Phillips says. "Reproductions are not usually as visually appealing. There is something magical about antique wood or vintage brass upholstery nails. Nothing new captures the romance, warmth and texture of the old. And antiques increase in value over time. When you bring home a reproduction, it simply becomes a used piece of furniture. It's like buying a new car instead of buying vintage. The value of the new car goes down considerably once you take it home, and it won't necessarily become a classic. And when it comes to antiques, the best part is that—unless you are buying really fine pieces—they are generally less expensive than good reproductions."

Given the clients' desire for a relaxing space in which to entertain family and friends, reproductions were sometimes used. "We didn't want to have anything that might detract someone from enjoying the home," says Phillips, who made sure the reproductions would blend well with the antiques.

The clients' mix of dark, English-style furniture and a soft color palette created a compelling decorative effect. "I love the contrast between dark furniture and flooring and light-toned architectural details," says Phillips. "It creates a dramatic silhouette, which has an interesting effect on the eye. The furniture has a stronger presence and rooms look as if they have more in them than they do." In short, spaces appear full, yet remain uncluttered and airy.

In this house, furniture selection was partly dictated by the rooms' high ceilings, which ranged from twelve to fourteen feet. To temper their scale, Phillips chose tall furniture, including antique chairs and armoires, and reproduction four-poster beds. "I personally hate filling up large spaces with huge sofas," he says. "Instead, I chose tall, sometimes overscaled pieces of wooden furniture. I also included tall-backed English chairs and large armoires. In new homes, good design is all about modulating scale."

## Architectural Details

Once fabric and furniture were taken care of, Phillips began sketching possible architectural details. "We wanted the interior shell to give the house a background with lots of character," the designer says. "Without the millwork, this home would have been just another beach house." Phillips designed it all—moldings, wainscoting, detailed ceilings—and had the elements custom-built on-site, where he could adjust their scale

The custom millwork that runs through this home can be clearly seen in these bathrooms. Phillips had it all handcrafted on-site, which gave him the opportunity to adjust the scale and proportions as the pieces were being made.

## DESIGNER TIPS

**Design with Antiques:** Antiques have a warmth and tactile quality that is hard to find in reproductions. They also add undeniable character to new rooms. Unless you are buying very high-end antiques, most are less expensive than good reproductions.

**Buy Solid Wood Furniture:** When buying reproductions, look for pieces made from solid wood. Avoid veneers. Look at furniture joints and avoid pieces that have been shoddily glued or nailed together. Tongue-and-groove joints are the best.

**Keep Furniture Consistent:** When purchasing reproductions, place the pieces you are considering next to actual antiques. (Some stores sell both new and old furniture. If the store allows returns, bring the reproductions home for a test.) If they look glaringly new, then they won't look appropriate in a home that also has antiques.

**Incorporate Architectural Details:** Interesting ceiling treatments help modulate the scale of large rooms. Their details add visual interest and distract from the rooms' height.

**Build High:** Tall ceiling heights are appealing in waterfront homes. They create a sense of airiness and reveal expansive views.

and proportions when necessary. "I prefer to install custom millwork in new homes when the budget allows," he says. "You just don't get the same effect when buying it out of a catalog."

The millwork included detailed ceiling treatments rarely seen in waterside homes. The clients, who were involved in every step of the design process, were eager to have them; Phillips liked the idea because the treatments would help temper the size of the rooms. "We wanted high ceilings so that we could build tall windows that looked out on the water," says Phillips. "They also give a sense of airiness and expansiveness, which is very nice in a waterfront home. But we didn't want the rooms to appear too tall or overpowering. The millwork reduces the scale, especially with the variety of architectural treatments we used."

In every room, Phillips installed "boxes" around the ceiling's support beams. A few rooms have additional treatments, including cross beams, bead board, planks and tray ceilings. "Those are the icing on the cake," the designer says.

The home's accessories include vintage nautical and beach-themed prints and advertisements. ("The artwork is non-confrontational," Phillips notes. "It adds soft touches.") There are also antique-looking ship models, lanterns and telescopes, and mounted reminders of fishing trips. But perhaps the most valuable accessories in the home are found in the husband's study, where Phillips installed state-of-the-art weather-tracking devices. The room is charmingly vintage, reminiscent of early 20th-century seaside weather stations. "The husband loves the command center," Phillips says. "He finds peace in knowing that he will be warned if a storm is bearing down on his home."

We can only hope this house has better luck with Mother Nature than its predecessor.

The fine details of antiques are clearly best seen when placed against simple backgrounds.

**Opposite:** These English-style bedposts are turned, like the legs of the table nearby. Turning is one of woodworking's oldest traditions—and in this setting, its fine detail can be appreciated. The dark wood is clearly outlined by the room's pale blues and the window's etheral glow.

# RESOURCES

**COMPANY IN FOCUS: ARCHITECTURAL PANELING** 1, 2

Architectural Paneling founder Anthony Lombardo is both a trained architect and a master woodworker. Over the past 40 years, his New York-based company has gained fame for its finely crafted wooden pieces, but it also sells paneling, cabinetry, moldings, fireplace surrounds and more to a global clientele. "We have had paneling installations in Tokyo, Brazil and Bermuda," Lombardo recalls. "We're like an 18th-century shop in that we make models of each project to ensure perfection for our clients." For inspiration, Lombardo travels to Europe, or visits the Metropolitan Museum of Art's period rooms. "I just got back from spending a week in Paris, where I visited several châteaux," he explains. "There is an art to their architectural details. Proportion is very important: You don't want moldings to look squat, or paneling to look skinny." Lombardo installs plain paneling so that clients can examine the wood grain, then lets them approve the color of the finish. "Finishes need to be tested, just as paint does," he says. "You need to sample an area first, and observe how light affects it." Architectural Paneling's catalog and website feature historically inspired woodwork pieces such as the Mantel WH2, based on a mantel in the White House State Dining Room, and Mantel 714, influenced by the delicate details of Robert Adam's design. Catalog items can be customized. **Call 212-371-9632 or visit www.apaneling.com.**

1.

2.

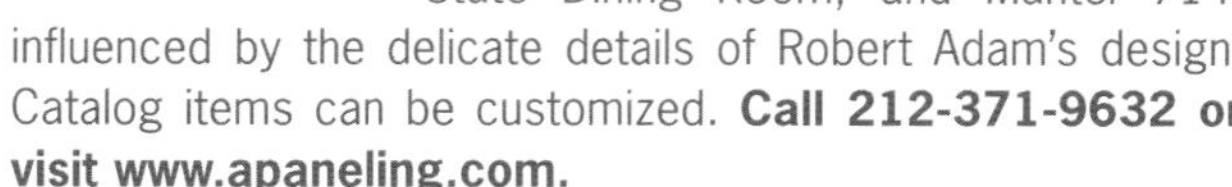

**ARTISANS: TANIA VARTAN** 3, 4

Two decades ago, Tania Vartan was in serious need of some direction. It was the early 1980s, and she had just decided to leave her job as a fashion designer to pursue a more artistic path. One day, famed interior designer Mark Hampton came to visit her apartment and was instantly impressed by the sprawling trompe l'oeil that decorated Vartan's walls. For the next two years, she would work only for him. "I owe everything to Mark Hampton," the artist remembers. "He gave me his top clients—including Lee Radziwill—and asked me to paint the rooms in his showhouse. I was so honored." Vartan has since gone on to great success, enriching the walls of many well-to-do clients with her "old-world trompe l'oeil," inspired by 18th- and 19th-century architectural decorative paintings. Nancy

3.

Reagan commissioned two of Vartan's life-sized murals for the inauguration of George H. W. Bush—a view of the circa-1920 White House state dining room, as seen through a set of mahogany doors, and a rendering of Teddy Roosevelt's children at play in the White House stairwells. (Both pieces now reside in the Smithsonian.)

After a decade of painting and running workshops in France, Vartan moved to Palm Beach, FL, where legendary British designer David Mlinaric (of Mlinaric, Henry and Zervudachi) recently commissioned her to do work for one of his clients. The new project involved painting seashells on hundreds of feet of canvas, which were then applied, like wallpaper, between a framework of architectural details. "The design was inspired by Emperor Frederick William II's library, in a palace in Potsdam, Germany," Vartan explains. "When placed between the moldings, cornice and wainscoting, it created a paneled effect , which was really interesting." Though known for her commissioned murals, the artist also does smaller, oil-on-canvas paintings, and offers workshops in Palm Beach and Siena and Florence, Italy. **Call 561-627-4848 or visit www.taniavartan.com.**

4.

**ARTISANS: CHUCK FISCHER** 5, 6

In 1980, after receiving a degree in fine arts from the University of Kansas, Chuck Fischer moved to Manhattan to pursue acting. To support himself, he accepted a decorative painting job from the legendary interior design firm Parish-Hadley. It was a defining decision: Fischer is now considered one of the finest decorative painters in the country, specializing in pastoral murals. "The early American primitive murals I paint are a reinterpretation of the itinerant 19th-century painters' murals," the artist says from his Manhattan studio. "My versions are more detailed, and have more depth, but they retain that quirky, whimsical, colorful look." Fischer also designs wallpaper and fabric for Brunschwig & Fils and Schumacher, and china patterns for Lenox, and has authored and illustrated two pop-up books for Rizzoli. "It's funny," he muses. "I never thought I'd be a painter." For an additional Fischer mural, see Chapter 6, *Twisted Traditional*. To the Trade. **Call 212-529-4953.**

5.

6.

## ARCHITECTURAL DETAILS

### BALMER ARCHITECTURAL MOULDINGS

In 1835, James Balmer established a plaster business in Cambridge, England. Sixty years later, his family moved to Toronto, where his descendants continue to run the company. Balmer Architectural Mouldings now supplements its plaster sales with polyurethane copies of architectural details, which are more affordable and easier to install. "All of our polyurethane molds are replicas of our plaster molds," says Dena Sicard, Balmer's Senior Marketing Coordinator. "The polyurethane is geared towards do-it-yourself types, while our plaster product is for the high-end market." Balmer's website features a catalog with 150 plaster and about 400 polyurethane products; an on-site library of over 12,000 patterns can be reviewed as inspiration for custom work.
**Call 800-665-3454 or visit www.balmer.com.**

## WALLPAPER

### GRACIE STUDIOS

Gracie Studios hand painted wallpaper is nothing less than spectacular. Each strip is produced in China by artisans under the direction of father and son, Brain and Mike Gracie, in a manner similar to how wallpaper was made in the 18th century. Patterns include Chinese scenes and continuous pattern, and Japanese, American and European scenes. Customization of the product is encouraged. "In the last few years, our business has changed," says Mike Gracie from their lower Manhattan workshop. "Today, clients want unique wallpapers so we work closely with them to tailor the designs." As a result of close collaboration with a variety of designers, the hues of a selection of Gracie's wallpapers have changed to reflect a more modern sensibility. These papers are more restrained in color, working well in traditional as well as contemporary settings. Gracie also sells Chinese and French antique wallpaper and antique and custom lacquer Asian furniture. Artisans in its Manhattan workroom paint a variety of murals on canvas and specialize in wallpaper and Japanese furniture restoration. Gracie Studio's products are sold through 9 To the Trade and retail showrooms in the U.S. **Call 212-924-6816 or visit www.graciestudio.com.**

### DESIGNERS GUILD

Award-winning British designer Tricia Guild creates wallpaper with a painterly quality, reminiscent of antique English styles. She draws inspiration from a wide variety of sources, including historic textile and wallpaper documents, Eastern decorative art and Italian architecture. But while her work is historically inspired, Guild's eclectic designs are fresh and lively, with exuberant-yet-sophisticated color combinations. Her company currently sells 2,000 wallpapers and coordinating textiles, with patterns ranging from printed florals and geometrics to checks and stripes. The La Desirase collection combines metallic accents with pastels, while a Carriacou pattern depicts a stylized English floral, and a Corak pattern features a cluster of silver motifs, inspired by a Malaysian design. In the U.S., you can find Guild products through Osborne & Little; a small sample can be viewed on its website, where there is a list of American showrooms. To the Trade. **Call 312-781-5695 or visit www.designersguild.com.**

### STARK WALLCOVERING

Stark has long been known for its carpets and textiles, but in 1998 it introduced wallpapers that were quickly embraced by the design community. The company's line ranges from archival document reproductions to loosely inspired, more contemporary works; hand-painted scenic styles feature chinoiserie to rival the 18th-century originals. Also stunning: The hand-blocked Adelphi, which duplicates popular Colonial patterns; Hamilton Urns, derived from a Boston paper stainer's stencil and offered in historically documented colorways; French Coffered, a dramatic and contemporary take on architectural details (which works as well in a traditional setting as in a modern one); and hand-screened, hand-glazed Italian Palazzo, with patterns inspired by an ornate, Renaissance-era inlaid Italian flooring. Stark's Dante wallpapers resemble an updated version of detailed marquetry, while its Savoye emulates an ornate wood veneer; Giardino combines ancient design motifs, such as damask and trellis, with novel materials such as grass cloth. Stark wallpapers can be viewed on the company website or at its 31 U.S. showrooms; many of its items can be customized. For more information about this source, see the sections on textiles and carpeting. To the Trade. **Call 212-355-7186 or visit www.dir-dd.com/stark-wallcovering.html.**

### ZOFFANY

Britain's Zoffany makes wallpaper inspired by antique motifs yet clever enough to suit both traditional and contemporary settings. Its Folio collection is based on an 18th-century Italian archival textile document; patterned with large-scale damask, it resembles a rich textile and makes walls seem almost upholstered. The Aubusson collection was also inspired by the same time period, with delicate floral patterns that recall traditional French carpets. The company's wallpaper motifs are oversized and attractively stylized, as shown by the RHS Florilegia collection: Inspired by the Royal Horticultural Society's botanical archives, it includes Macao, a lovely, three-dimensional floral pattern. Zoffany welcomes orders for customization, and also sells coordinating fabrics. Collections can be seen on its website and in showrooms across the country. To the Trade. **Call 800 395 8760 or visit www.zoffany.com.**

### WAVERLY

F. Schumacher's Waverly brand offers inexpensive and attractive versions of historically inspired wallpapers. The brand is ideal for do-it-yourself types: An interactive website lets you see how its 4,000+ patterns would look in various settings. Order samples and products online, or consult the list of U.S. showrooms. Retail. **Visit www.waverly.com.**

## PAINT

### BENJAMIN MOORE

For years, Benjamin Moore has been considered the market's best. The company recently introduced two-ounce sample jars of its most popular colors, which contain enough paint to apply two coats to an area of four square feet. Store locations are listed on its website. Retail. **Visit www.benjaminmoore.com.**

### DONALD KAUFMAN

Donald Kaufman works as a color consultant to top-shelf architects and designers such as Philip Johnson. He also produces his own line of paint, which designers credit with having a unique luminosity. (The secret: A generous helping of transparent pigments, which reflect light rather than absorb it.) Kaufman's paints can be found at The Color Factory, Ring's End, Santa Monica Painter's Supply and Cox Paint. Oversized paint chips and sample-sized pints are also available. Retail. **Call 212-594-2608.**

### FARROW & BALL

Founded in the mid-20th century, this legendary English company manufactures paint using traditional methods and secret, original formulas. It developed the first paint colors for the United Kingdom's National Trust, and still includes those hues in the 132 paint shades it offers. Designers praise Farrow & Ball for its depth of color and lack of odor, which makes it easier for their clients to move in quickly. The company sells sample pots of paint, which cover five square feet of space with two coats. A fan deck paint book is also available. Retail. **Call 888-511-1121 or visit www.farrow-ball.com.**

### PRATT & LAMBERT

Designers recommend Pratt & Lambert paint for its excellent quality and color. Now owned by Sherwin-Williams, the company was founded over 150 years ago in Buffalo, NY, and is currently sold through 1,000+ U.S. retailers. Its Ovation™ faux finishes and tools offer foolproof instructions that show you how to create 15 styles, including faux suede and color glazes. Retail. **Call 800-289-7728 or visit www.prattandlambert.com.**

### DUNN-EDWARDS

Los Angeles-based Dunn-Edwards has been manufacturing high-quality paint for over 75 years. It sells its products through 70 of its own outlets in the western U.S., where it can match paint colors to just about anything a customer brings in—fabric, wallpaper and more. Retail. **Call 888-337-2468 or visit www.dunnedwards.com.**

### SCHREUDER

Holland is the birthplace of the paint industry and home to Schreuder, which concocts its paint using a centuries-old formula. Designers praise Schreuder's high-quality finish and depth of color. Available in the U.S. through Fine Paints of Europe, it also offers sample pots for those early trials. Retail. **Call 800-332-1556 or visit www.finepaintsofeurope.com.**

### OLD-FASHIONED MILK PAINT

The Old-Fashioned Milk Paint Company of Groton, MA, manufactures authentic Colonial and Shaker milk paint using the same basic ingredients as our forefathers used: milk protein, lime and earth pigments. Paints come in powdered form and are easily liquefied; there are 16 early American colors, which may be combined with a base to form other hues. The company also offers pint-sized powder packages for testing, and a brochure with paint chips. Available in Groton and through 400 U.S. dealers. Retail. **Call 866-350-6455 or visit www.milkpaint.com.**

GLENN GISSLER



# CHAPTER 5

# REFINED RUSTIC

With an architecture degree from the Rhode Island School of Design and a broad knowledge of antiques, design history and art, Glenn Gissler is as skilled at building "newly old" homes as he is at re-decorating a space to remove the generic stamp of the builders' home. In his experience, the latter is often the bigger challenge. "Many of these new homes don't have a soul," Gissler laments from his Manhattan office. "They don't have a personality. All they have is square footage. People who come to me are desperate for change."

The designer's admiration for objects from earlier time periods is obvious in all of the homes he decorates. As a young adult, Gissler collected architectural fragments, including newel posts and column capitals. Now he focuses on artifacts that predate Christ. "I personally like to have a little B.C. in a room," Gissler says. "My wife and I collect contemporary art, and I like having things with the collection that add a little history. Everything that is new is an outgrowth of something that preceded it. Otherwise, we are living in a vacuum."

Although the rooms Gissler designs look organic and unforced, a rich layering process goes into creating them. For the home pictured in this chapter—a dwelling near Westhampton Beach, New York—Gissler needed to eliminate all the builders' details, from the doors and fixtures to the sheetrock walls and fireplace surround. "There was no dimension, no texture and no style to it," the designer remembers. He had to find a way to enhance the structure's bones, then just choose the right furnishings and decorative touches to finish it off.

Gissler added beams, a large wooden antique chandelier and heavy, grounding furniture to tame the height of the 18-foot ceiling in the living room.

## Enhancing the Bones

Gissler began by making architectural changes. To balance the asymmetry of the exterior, he added more windows to several rooms and replaced the sliding doors with French ones that matched the original window frames. "As a 21st-century builder's home, the house didn't have any architectural integrity," Gissler says. "But by creating balance and consistency in the façade, we were able to give the house a sense of architecture that it was lacking."

To create interest on the inside, Gissler added Shaker-style moldings and beams throughout the home, then painted them a taupe color to contrast with its cream-colored walls. Shaker architecture and furniture is marked by quality workmanship, straight lines and little decorative detailing, all of which gave a sense of craftsmanship to this home's formerly generic interior. Although Shaker furnishings often come in

This newly-built stone fireplace dominates the living room, adding shadows and dimension to the room.

DESIGNER TIPS

**Symmetry Matters:** Add architectural integrity to generic builders' homes by creating symmetrical façades. If the doors and window frames don't match, replace them so that they do. A home shouldn't look like a hodgepodge of styles.

**Architectural Elements:** Add moldings and beams to rooms without them. If the house is meant to be casual, choose simple Shaker-style moldings.

**Optical Illusions:** In double-height rooms, add large antique or reproduction chandeliers. Hang them down about ten feet. They help make large, open ceilings feel less towering.

**Keep Floors Consistent:** Use one flooring material in the public rooms to give a sense of continuity. Contrasting floors tend to chop up rooms.

**Door Solutions:** To give a new space immediate character, replace cheap, hollow doors with solid, high-quality wooden ones. The doors you choose should echo the style of your home and be used throughout it.

bright colors, Gissler choose to keep the hues muted here.

He recalls his first impression of the place. "The rooms were plain sheetrock and completely lifeless without moldings or beams. "But with this type of home, we didn't want highly ornamental details either. What were needed were flat architectural elements. They added the dimension and shadow that brought the rooms to life."

The moldings and beams also helped bring a large room down to size. "There was a problematic double-height ceiling in the living room," Gissler remembers. "It was 18 feet tall. To bring the scale down, we added the architectural elements and a large 19th-century wooden chandelier. They eliminated the awkward feel of the room."

Gissler also added extra doors, replacing the originals with simple Shaker-style versions. It was an easy way to breathe life into the house. "There was no weight or dimension to them," he says of the originals. "And some openings had no doors at all, which created empty, lifeless gaps in the home."

In the public rooms, Gissler removed all the floor tiles and replaced them with dark wood. "Having some rooms tiled and others wooden can chop up a home," he says. "Using one flooring material brought a greater sense of continuity—and the wood added warmth." As a crowning touch, Gissler used area rugs made from sea grass and sisal, a strong Mexican fiber.

In the living room, the designer replaced an uninspired sheetrock fireplace surround with a fieldstone façade that ran from floor to ceiling. The new fireplace was made from Connecticut fieldstone and was built in the "dry stack" method, where the mortar is not seen. A bluestone slate slab served as a mantel.

"I love the drystack method of fireplace-building,

When framed properly, even common garden ferns take on a delicate, intriguing beauty.

*"I am pretty obsessive about* ***light*** *fixtures. I think they are a real opportunity to bring* ***character*** *to a space. They can really* ***enhance*** *or support the architecture."*

In the den, Gissler uses an African tribal dress as art. Its texture and abstract pattern enrich the room's rustic-yet-exotic design scheme.

because it creates so many shadows and adds so much texture," Gissler says. "What many of these new homes lack are shadows and texture. Everything is so flat."

To retrofit the house with a sense of history, Gissler then added clapboard shingles on one wall in the dining room, making the room appear to be a late addition. "In older homes, you can see where changes were made," he says. "For example, a wall may have exterior cladding that shows where the house used to stop. That aspect of an older home is charming, and when added to a new home, it brings charm with it."

## Rustic-on-Rustic Furnishings

In the living room and kitchen/dining area, Gissler installed a mix of antique and custom-made light fixtures (the latter including the dining room chandelier and kitchen wall sconces). "I am pretty obsessive about light fixtures," he says. "I think they are a real opportunity to bring character to a space. They can really enhance or support the architecture."

Budget limitations affected Gissler's choice of furnishings. Unlike some of the homes he decorates, this one would not be filled with fine antiques and artwork; rather it would derive charm from its unusual art and furniture. "The basic design concept of the home was rustic-on-rustic," Gissler recalls. "The furniture, fabric, lighting and decorative accessories were all rustic, but in different ways, which created interest. What tied everything together—in addition to unpretentious rusticity—was the muted color scheme and dark brown wooden furniture."

Gissler filled the rooms with furniture that was a combination of styles, largely British colonial, Anglo Raj, South American and 19th-century American. British colonial furniture, loosely based on the historic Regency style, is generally

This kitchen was completely gutted and rebuilt in a nod to early American Shaker style. The flat molding, in a contrasting color, adds needed dimension to the room.

made of dark wood and combined with cane, wicker or leather inserts. It was originally designed to be portable enough to travel with the English soldiers who ventured off on campaigns during the 19th-century expansion of the British Empire.

Arriving in the midst of the British colonial movement, Anglo Raj furniture was designed during England's occupation of India and tends to combine traditional British and Indian designs. Known for its exceptional craftsmanship, Anglo Raj is distinguished from other English styles by its use of exotic woods and rich carvings.

"These Third World pieces are less formal and more charming than many English pieces," says Gissler. "They were hand-carved by local craftsmen who were interpreting furniture styles exported from England. The net result is a recognizable and traditional furniture form—with a twist. It works well for people who want a traditional point of view but don't want 'formal.'"

The South American furniture is hand-hewn, giving it an instant patina. It tends to be heavy and durable—perfect for rustic interiors. It's also relatively inexpensive. The early American Colonial furniture posseses simplified forms,

**Opposite:** Adding an extra row of windows (on the bottom) really opened up this informal dining area. The room's other highlights include an antique Anglo Raj table, a British colonial dining chair and a wrought-iron chandelier from the 1920s.

**Above:** This formal dining area has one wall made of clapboard siding to make the room seem like an addition. The oil-rubbed bronze light fixture is a Gissler design (executed by artisan Daniel Berglund) that evokes 19th-century lamps.

DESIGNER TIPS

**The Natural Focal Point:** Hire a mason to build an impressive fireplace with aged-looking stone. Fireplaces are often the most natural focal point in a room, and if done well, they can give a room immediate presence.

**Retrofitting History:** Exterior shingles or clapboard on one wall will give the impression that the room was an addition to an earlier structure. Because Colonial homes grew as families grew, older homes are filled with rooms like this.

**Fabric and Artwork:** Collect fabrics and art that follow the interior design scheme. Woven fabrics, velvets and leathers are rich in texture and enrich new spaces, while black- and-white photographs and antique engravings can be inexpensive old world additions to your home.

**Furnishings:** Buy antique or reproduction furniture to enhance the effect of Third World antiques—or try newly hand-constructed furniture from South America. There is a rusticity to these types of furniture that helps age a home.

Gissler's tabletops are rich in variety and texture. He had the lamp cast himself, while the framed engraving—which demonstrates how to build an obelisk—is a relic from the 18th-century.

offering a subtle contrast with most furniture choices.

Although he bought a few key pieces at fine antiques stores, Gissler largely visited lesser antiques shops, junk emporiums and specialty stores that carried South American, Far Eastern and Indian furniture and objects. One of the most special pieces he found was the armoire now in the home's living room. Nearly ten feet tall, the 18th-century Italian antique serves as a high-end TV stand and balances out the floor-to-ceiling fireplace on the other side of the room.

For fabrics, Gissler and his clients settled on "simple, earthy" selections, including natural-colored weaves and plush materials such as antique linen velvet and leather. "All the fabrics carry a lack of pretension," the designer says.

The artwork, which Gissler bought specifically for this home, includes framed antique engravings and photographs, and traditional African garb. "In the den, we hung a tribal dress from Zaire over the sofa," Gissler says. "It looks like abstract Western art, and adds more history and texture to the room."

Gissler's tabletop designs further demonstrate the complexity at play in his rooms. Atop one rustic Third World cabinet in the living room, there is a wooden lamp Gissler had made from an antique casting mold. A simply matted and framed print leans against the wall, while a short, thin, silver-plated square cup is used as a flower vase. In front of the vase sits a low, flat ceramic bowl that Gissler calls "hippie art from the 1970s." Two stacked books complete the scene.

"I approach designing a tabletop vignette in the same manner that I do a home," Gissler explains. "The concepts are similar. You just need a variation of scale and texture and styles for it to be successful."

Complex design schemes never looked so easy.

Gissler says that this home once lacked architectural integrity. The designer remedied the problem by adding French doors and matching windows, both of which gave it a sense of balance.

# LIGHT FIXTURES

1.

2.

3.

4.

5.

## DESIGNER TIPS: CHARACTER WITH LIGHT FIXTURES BY GLENN GISSLER 1

*I am pretty obsessive about lighting, as I think it offers a real opportunity to bring character into a space. Here's how to use decorative light fixtures to enhance and support the design scheme of a home:*

**Highlight your style:** Whether antique or reproduction, light fixtures should be touchstones for the entire home's design. Crystal chandeliers that look like they belong in Versailles should not be hung in suburban dwellings. You may want your visitors to leave with an impression of grandeur, but if your home isn't a palace, a chandelier isn't going to turn it into one. An attractive antique brass chandelier is more appropriate.

**Bring the scale down:** Fixtures make large rooms seem more intimate. If a space has 15-foot ceilings and you hang a large chandelier so that it drops down nine feet, you bring the eye down with it. This visual trick will make the room feel less overpowering (one reason why you often find large hanging lights in double-height foyers). Light fixtures have even been used to break up sound and reduce echoes in large spaces.

**Complement the architecture:** Fixtures help establish scale, while their light helps create an ambience. As a result, the light you use should be different in each room of your house. Installing dimmers lets you choose an appropriate amount of light for different times of the day. At night, dimmers in bathrooms and kitchens are essential, as they keep you from walking in the dark or in super-bright light to get a drink of water.

**Provide general illumination:** I like to mount small frosted glass fixtures on the walls, just beneath the ceilings, to provide general illumination and cast light on artwork and mantels. I'll also surface-mount subtle versions of mono points (individual track fixtures), then add hanging lights and table and floor lamps. I'll even place lights under kitchen cabinets to illuminate counters, which need to be bright when you're preparing food. But I avoid using recessed lights at all costs, as they darken the ceiling plane while illuminating the floor. Puncturing ceilings with recessed lights also has a cheapening effect, exposing the thinness of sheetrock—certainly something to steer clear of if you are trying to infuse a new space with old world charm.

**One last note:** Avoid lacquered brass light fixtures. Their color never mellows, and they look like cheap gold.

**ARTISANS: DANIEL BERGLUND** 1, 2, 3

Daniel Berglund's colorful resumé includes designing set and light fixtures for Manhattan nightclubs, but the artisan is just as well-known for the pieces he creates in his Lyme, CT studio. A favorite of designers Clodagh, Glenn Gissler and Sam Robin, Berglund first made a splash with his large, cylindrical light columns back in the 1980s. Today he turns out industrial-looking chandeliers, sconces and lamps as well-suited to Arts and Crafts-inspired homes as to chic restaurants. "Nothing currently popular inspires me," Berglund says. "I am mostly influenced by the early 20th-century Austrian architect Otto Wagner and the more industrial-looking design of the Art Nouveau period. I translate the feeling of that time into light fixtures."

Berglund uses exotic vintage metals—such as jet engine parts—to give his fixtures an aged appearance. "Some of the parts have been tortured for years by high heat," he says. "They have a patina of age. If they aren't distressed, I age them with chemicals or wire brushes." The process adds an appealing warmth to the industrial materials, while the fixtures' elegantly odd composition make them seem both beautiful and familiar. In addition to Berglund's own creations, he also collaborates with designers to fashion fixtures to their specifications. Image number 1 is an example of a collaboration with designer Glenn Gissler. For more examples of Berglund's work, see Chapter 5, *Refined Rustic*. To the Trade. **Call 860-434-5162.**

**ARTISANS: GATES MOORE LIGHTING** 4, 5

Patricia Moore works in a charming early 20th-century barn in the historic Silvermine area of Norwalk, CT, where she churns out antique-looking fixtures and restores antique lights. The property has been in her family's hands since 1917, but it's not the only thing Moore inherited: Her cluttered workroom is a testament to the craftsmanship and dedication she learned from her father, the late Kevin Gates Moore. In 1938, he founded this family business, which daughter Moore has now run for almost two decades, side–by–side with craftsman William Castro. Their workshop brims with lamp parts, lanterns and tools, some of which date back to the 1800s.

Moore and Castro's light fixtures are handcrafted using old-fashioned techniques, which perfectly complement their early American style. "A lot of fixtures made today look cheap to me," Moore explains. "The attention to detail just isn't there." She and Castro bend and crimp metal pieces with simple hand tools, then solder the joined parts together. The wood used in their fixtures is always hand-turned, and the finishes are also applied by hand. Even the faux candles are handmade! Fixtures can be painted, oxidized or distressed to a client's specifications. "I compare it to the way seamstresses work," Moore says. "We trace patterns and cut them out of metal (or hand-turn the wood), then hem the edges. Our items are unique, well-constructed and durable. They are crafted the way all things used to be—with care." Catalogs available. Retail. **Call 203-847-3231 or visit www.gatesmoorelighting.com.**

**COMPANY IN FOCUS: URBAN ARCHAEOLOGY** 6, 7

Urban Archaeology began as a salvage company about 25 years ago. In the early 1990s, top designers such as Carl D'Aquino and Victoria Hagen often visited the firm, placing large orders for vintage items. But when founder Gil Shapiro discovered that he didn't have enough pieces to fill some of the orders, he was forced to get creative: "A designer would ask for nine lamps when we only had two authentic matches," he remembers. "We decided to make reproductions based on their requests. Now we are largely a reproduction company with some salvaged pieces."

Urban Archaeology's fixtures come in a wide range of styles, including Art Deco, Mission and Victorian. They have been modeled after everything from a hanging light on an early 20th-century ship (inspiration for the company's nautical Cargo Pendant) to a 1920s fixture found in an airport hanger (template for the Double Prismatic). All of the fixtures are handcrafted by a bevy of artisans—from ironworkers to pattern and moldmakers—and a variety of finishes is available. Shapiro also has a team of five designers who reinterpret vintage pieces. The fixtures are generally made in his seven-story loft in Manhattan's TriBeCa neighborhood, but Urban Archaeology has several East Coast showrooms and 90 U.S. and Canadian distributors. For more about this source, see the section on plumbing. Retail and To the Trade. **Call 212-431-4646 or visit www.urbanarchaeology.com.**

6.

7.

1.

2.

3.

4.

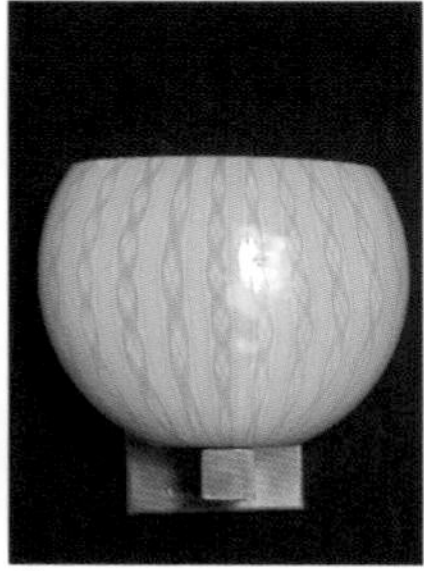

5. 6. 7.

*Light fixtures are often called "jewelry for the home." They brighten up dark rooms and add sparkle and interest to bland ones. When creating a space with old-world charm, choose antique fixtures that have been wired with electricity or find well-constructed reproductions—and remember that your choice of lampshade must also strike the correct period note. Here are some of the market's best lighting sources, including a few that specialize in shades.*

**145 ANTIQUES**

145 Antiques was recently named the best source for chandeliers by *House & Garden* magazine, where it also made the top 10 for best overall lighting. Located in Manhattan's Chelsea neighborhood, 145 offers a wide selection of vintage and antique European fixtures, with styles ranging from 1920s Art Deco to 1970s contemporary. Founder Gerald Barnard opened the store after living for 15 years in Paris, where he ran a booth in the city's Clignancourt flea market. He also produces his own line of reproduction furniture with co-owner Jim Gurski; called Re-Editions, it is largely inspired by French Deco and the Napoleon III period. The store is also an excellent source for antique furniture and decorative accessories, especially mirrors. All pieces can be found on the company website. Retail. **Call 212-807-1149 or visit www.145antiques.com.**

**LAMPWORKS** 1, 2

"I used to get so frustrated, because I couldn't find the fixtures I wanted in the marketplace," remembers Bébé Regnier, a former interior designer and owner of Lampworks. "I decided to start a company that could provide designers with exactly what they need." It was a savvy, and profitable, plan: Industry folks now flock to her custom lighting store, bringing pictures or drawings of items they want replicated. "We have 50 small vendors and artisans who produce lights and lighting components exclusively for us," Regnier says. In addition to reproduction and restored antique fixtures, the store sells custom and ready-made shades. Most of the business is residential, but the company also supplies commercial venues such as Saks Fifth Avenue, and staffers recently restored the early 20th-century lights in Manhattan's historic Algonquin Hotel. A sampling of Lampworks' products can be seen on its website, while more are on view at its Upper East Side showroom. Clients include Randy Ridless, Scott Salvator and James Rixner. To the Trade and Retail. **Call 212-750-1500 or visit www.lampworksinc.com.**

**ORIENTAL LAMP SHADE CO.** 3, 4
For the last 85 years, the family-run Oriental Lamp Shade Company has been handcrafting traditional shades and running a full-service lamp shop. They sell a wide variety of ready-made light fixtures and lamp parts (including jade and brass finials), and can turn almost anything into a lamp, including the vases and urns they sell on-site. The company's design consultants can suggest period-specific lampshades for an old light or help update a cherished antique with an unusual cover. For custom shades, check out Oriental Lamp Shade's website or one of its two Manhattan stores. Retail. **Call 212-832-8190 or visit www.orientallampshade.com.**

**CHAMELEON** 5, 6, 7
Robert Degiarde and John Harvey founded Chameleon 11 years ago, shortly after receiving their MBAs. The duo now has a 4,000-square-foot shop dedicated to antique light fixtures and "faithful" reproductions, which they make in several sizes. "There is so much new construction that involves tall ceiling heights," Harvey explains from his Manhattan store. "Clients need large fixtures that are proportionate to their rooms." Styles are diverse, ranging from Colonial to rococo and Anglo-Indian, but they're all beautiful. Retail. **Call 212-355-6300 or visit www.chameleonsoho.com.**

**CHARLES EDWARDS**
Serendipity played a large part in Charles Edwards' decision to start a lighting business. As the story goes, Edwards was selling antique furniture and accessories in his London store, and was trying to figure out a way to maximize the ceiling space. He started carrying light fixtures, which soon caught the eye of designer David Easton. Easton asked Edwards to copy some of his lanterns, and a wildly successful reproduction business was born. The hanging and wall-mounted lanterns are inspired by 19th- and 20th-century English and French designs; some are distressed to look antique, while others update traditional forms. Edwards' website lists U.S. showrooms that carry his products. A catalog is also available. Retail. **Call 011 44 020 7736 8490 or visit www.charlesedwards.com.**

**CRISTAL**
Fort Worth, TX-based Cristal has been producing light fixtures for just two decades, but the company's products already seem like antiques. Inspired by historical pieces, these high-end stunners rely on ancient techniques such as lost wax and brass casting, and are carefully made by artisans in 55 factories around the world. Some models take months, such as the Aslan chandelier, which is based on a 19th-century Regency fixture: Its metal is shaped with wax, while its finish requires 15 different treatments. A glass Veneta chandelier, produced on the Italian island of Murano, is just as brilliantly crafted: It's dipped in 24-karat gold powder for a luxe look. Retail. **Call 888-399-4947 or visit www.cristal-usa.com.**

## LAMPSHADES

**SHADES FROM THE MIDNIGHT SUN**
Before opening Shades from the Midnight Sun, owner Sue Wellott was head of merchandising for men's shirts at Pierre Cardin. Her background in fashion and textiles certainly shows: Many designers consider Wellott's Bronxville, NY, company to be the best source for high-end custom shades. "Designers can either choose from our trims and fabrics or bring in their own," says Wellott, who works with a staff of seven. "We will make shades to their specifications." To the Trade. **Call 914-779-7237.**

**TRANS-LUXE**
"Shades are the new light fixtures," proclaims trans-LUXE co-founder Fernando Santangelo. "They are no longer just an accessory to a lamp. They can be the lamp." Santangelo and his partner Sandra Santos have been making custom lampshades for nearly a decade; before opening their store in Manhattan's SoHo neighborhood, both were involved in interior design. "If you use a traditionally shaped lampshade as a fixture, you are able to update a historic look while still retaining the impression of the style," Santangelo says. All of trans-LUXE's lampshades are made by hand in its basement workroom, down to their metal frames. "We fabricate everything," Santangelo explains. "We make the shades to the customers' specifications, then hand-sew the fabric and trim." Styles range from mid-20th-century modern to baroque and Middle Eastern, with some inspired by Fortuny's lanterns. Customers supply their own fabric and trim or choose from a vast selection (linen, silks, cottons and more); design books are available for historical inspiration. trans-LUXE also sells lamps, lamp parts, reproduction finials and decorative chains imported from Europe. Additionally, the team can suggest appropriate lampshades for vintage or antique lights, and rewire problematic fixtures. Retail. **Call 212-925-5863.**

SCOTT SALVATOR



# CHAPTER 6

# TWISTED TRADITIONAL

Given that the people who seek out Scott Salvator to decorate their homes frequently have royal titles, his firm's design tends to have an aristocratic air to it. "We don't design for Prince, we design for Prince Someone," jokes Salvator from his Upper East Side Manhattan office.

Salvator, part of a family that has worked in construction and historical restoration for three generations, was trained in design at FIT and Parsons, and is well versed in the history of design. After working with industry legends like Mario Buatta and Robert Metzger, Salvator started his own firm more than a decade ago. Shortly afterwards, he was joined by Michael Zabriskie, who had worked for some of the same designers Salvator had. The two have been working side-by-side ever since.

At a time when many designers are accused of simply *styling* rooms rather than designing them, Salvator stands apart. Each of his spaces is highly detailed and brimming with an eclectic collection of antiques and *objets d'art*. "The problem with so much of design today is that designers are more stylists than

**Opposite:** In this designer showhouse room, a simple stone mantel is surrounded by distressed mirrors from floor to ceiling, making the space seem older and larger. An unusual early 20th-century framed blue Venetian mirror, placed over a reflective wall, is a signature Salvator design element. The 19th-century Baroque-styled cabinet and the 18th-century upholstered armchair are Russian. **Above:** This 19th-century black lacquered English chest, on a stand, is balanced by two leafy palms, which add an exotic element to the traditional English-styled room. Antique accessories and paintings, which the clients collected during their travels, add symmetry.

**Think Traditional, with a Twist:** Traditional design, when done well, is timeless. But add curious elements to traditional rooms to make them interesting. Add the unexpected, like seashells in formal apartments, or elaborate chandeliers in country homes.

**Create a Great Base:** Use architectural elements such as paneling and molding to create a foundation of order and symmetry in a room.

**Use Gem Tones:** To create regal rooms, paint and lacquer the walls in gem tones, including ruby red, sapphire blue, emerald green and amethyst purple. The tones are dark and add warmth, depth and drama.

**Hang Rich Wallpaper:** The right wallpapers, such as those with chinoiserie patterns, age a room instantly. Wallpaper also helps to make a room feel full when it still needs a few pieces of furniture.

**Make Your New Moldings Old:** To remove the hard, too-perfect edge of new machine-made moldings, apply a cheesecloth stipple over the base coat of paint. All molding used to be made of plaster or handcrafted—the stipple gives a bit of patina by adding imperfection to the new surfaces.

decorators," he laments. "They create stage sets. There is no layering, and when that is done in a brand-new space, the room will never feel antique."

As Salvator sees it, every aspect of a room has to be considered before one can attempt to create an old world sensibility. "All the areas of the room need to be addressed before it can look fabulous," he says. "One must make the room complete, before it can even begin to be interesting. One great piece of art will not make a great room."

The firm's style is lavish and layered, with an eclectic mix of Continental pieces. The spaces in this chapter demonstrate the firm's versatility, ranging from city apartments and country homes to designer showhouses. "We design in a classic way because it rarely ages if done well," Salvator says. "Traditional design is timeless—and for our clients, it can be more socially acceptable. Also, traditional is a better overall value: Antiques and art appreciate."

## Finding a Twist

Salvator rooms are traditional but, delightfully, there is always a twist to them. The firm adds whimsical elements that give their rich rooms a bit of humor. "I don't want my rooms to be heavy-handed or tired," the designer says. "Hopefully, they are colorful, amusing and inviting."

The whimsy is added with elements such as palm trees and seashells in Park Avenue apartments, and blood red chinoiserie secretaries or fanciful Venetian chandeliers in country homes. These classically-designed rooms also boast lots of mirrors—on the walls, on the furniture, even layered over one another. The combined effect is one of magic and glamour.

"I like to think of our design as MGM-meets-Park-Avenue-meets-Palm-Beach," Salvator says. "Escapism is important to us. We love to create rooms that take you to another place just, as a movie should. Fantasy combined with uncommon or unexpected items is wonderful. There is nothing worse than being common—just look at cars today, compared with cars of the early 1960s. There is no style, no flair. It's a Gap world."

Cherry blossom wallpaper gives this dining room an elegant period look. The banquette was modeled after one in the Duke and Dutchess of Windsor's private collection. The gilded antique wall sculpture is Rococo in style and supports a collection of blue and white export porcelain.

The firm frequently starts a project with a blank slate, often when a full gut is needed. "It's nice when rooms have great architectural detailing," Salvator says. "But, sadly, in new construction, they usually don't—and there is often an abundance of 'built-ins.' Architects just don't know when to stop inserting them."

Their first step generally is to send the built-ins "out the door" and design the architectural details they think will properly enhance the room. Salvator favors English-inspired architectural elements, which create a foundation of order and symmetry in rooms. "A strong architectural shell is needed in all of our rooms," he explains. "It provides the base."

## An Uncommon Touch

Salvator likes to use decorative tricks to give his designs what he calls "the bittersweet quality of fallen aristocracy." To create this aged, upscale look, he chooses strong color, antique-looking wallpaper and textiles, formally-designed curtains, curvaceous upholstered pieces and antiques. "We are not the designers to call if you want a contemporary, beige interior," Salvator emphasizes. "We love color, intricate wallpaper, elaborate chandeliers, *objets d'art* and an abundance of pillows. We like pattern on top of pattern."

Salvator's color palette is large, and he chooses color based on the client's preferences and their complexion. "My clients have to look attractive in their own homes," the designer explains. When he wants to create a regal feeling in a room, he uses gem tones such as ruby red, sapphire blue, emerald green and amethyst purple. "Gem tones add depth, warmth and drama," Salvator says. "I like to lacquer a room with them because it lends an antique feeling to a room."

While interior design magazines are heralding the return of wallpaper, where Salvator's concerned, they're just preaching to the choir: He never stopped using it. "Wallpaper lends another layer of warmth and detail to a room," he says. "I don't buy that 'my grandmother had wallpaper, so I can't have it' nonsense. Wallpaper often looks like it has been in a room for a long time, which helps a new space look older. It decorates a

To update and highlight the existing oak paneling (which had been painted white), Salvator had custom painters stain it a creamy taupe color and applied an exotic-looking grain. Paneling generally gives a richness and warmth to rooms that sheetrock can't.

**Previous Page:** Famed muralist Chuck Fischer painted the walls to depict a pastoral scene that mimics the home's surroundings, but imagines the landscape as it would have looked a few centuries earlier. The front of the dining chairs are upholstered with a faux animal print; the backs use the same check pattern as the window treatments. The mural and various patterns, including the sisal area rug topped off with an antique Aubusson rug, create a space with rich, yet interesting texture. **Above:** These creamy white doors are accented with gilt, the perfect complement to a high-style, English-inspired dining room. Antiques enhance the historical spirit evoked by the room's classic architecture.

*"All the areas of the room need to be addressed before it can look **fabulous**. One must make the room **complete**, before it can even begin to be **interesting**. One great piece of **art** will not make a **great room**."*

room like wrapping paper decorates a present."

Salvator frequently uses wallpaper in dining rooms—often chinoiserie patterns that recall England's 19th-century fascination with the Far East. "Wallpaper is a traditional European design element," he says. "And it's great for young people on a budget who can't fill an entire room all at once. In short, it's an inexpensive way to remove the emptiness of a new space."

In addition to wallpaper, Salvator uses faux painting and finishing techniques to add character to a room. On new wooden moldings, he has artisans apply a cheese cloth stipple over the base coat. "It takes away that sharp, too-perfect edge and makes moldings appear more like aged plaster," the designer says.

Salvator also uses faux painting techniques to create wood and marble grains that are either too expensive or impossible to find. "Sometimes a new, mahogany library looks no better than a roomful of kitchen cabinets," Salvator says. "To differentiate a room and give it an old world feeling, we duplicate exotic woods and hard-to-find marbles. It adds another layer of sophistication and interest to the space."

The designer always includes mirrors as architectural elements in city apartments, a trick he learned as a child when visiting the historic 18th-century home of English architect Sir John Sloane. "No matter how big they are, Manhattan apartments are never big enough—and they never have enough light, unless they are in contemporary buildings," Salvator says. "Mirrors expand a room and reflect more light, which brightens them up."

Antiques are another essential part of Salvator's newly old rooms. He rarely buys reproduction furniture, and focuses on antiques that range from Regency to Art Deco, with an emphasis on English, Italian and Russian pieces. "Antiques are

**Top:** When Salvator installs large expanses of mirrors, he always hangs artwork or antique mirrors on top of them and frequently installs light fixtures into them to mitigate any coolness.

**Bottom:** Rich architectural details, including an impressive staircase mated with antique accessories—gilded mirrors, a wall clock and a crystal chandelier—gives this expansive space an old world impression but one that has been refreshingly updated.

If these walls had simply been painted, this would have been just another antiques-filled foyer. Salvator created excitement by covering one wall with a mirror, which enlivens all the elements in the room—including the floor's antique marble diamond pattern, distressed cabinet and Chinese Chippendale-style bamboo chairs.

DESIGNER TIPS

**Paint Faux Patterns:** Faux painting exotic wood and marble patterns on wooden paneling and built-ins sets them apart from common paneling.

**Hang Costly Fabrics, Upholster with Durable Ones:** Use expensive fabric for the window treatments and less expensive and more durable fabric as upholstery. Spend money on things that people don't come in contact with and be sensible about the items that will be used daily.

**Try Mirrors:** Mirrors can be used as architectural elements. They are especially good to use in small residences with little light. Mirrors help expand rooms, reflect views and increase the amount of light.

**Adapt Curtain Heft:** Adjust your curtain choices to the style of the room. In bedrooms, install soft curtains; in living rooms, hang heavier, more stiffly designed ones.

**Find the Right Professional:** If you want elaborate, antique-inspired curtains, find a good designer, seamstress or workroom. Most workrooms make good curtain panels, but you must find the right person to make beautiful valences and jabots.

**Use Reproductions for Dining Chairs:** Antiques are an essential way to add character to new rooms and are a better value than reproductions—except when it comes to dining chairs. These chairs should be well proportioned to suit your family and guests. Also, you can buy as many reproduction chairs as you need, while it is often hard to find eight to twelve matching antique chairs.

almost always preferable to reproductions, as they are a better value," he says. "With one exception: Reproduction dining chairs. These chairs are almost always better to buy because they are bigger and stronger than antiques, and you can buy as many as you need."

Although Salvator's rooms look antique, and are highly decorated (lending them that 'roped-off' feeling), he designs all of his rooms with the hope that they will be used frequently. To create old world-looking rooms that are user friendly, he carefully chooses the types of fabric to upholster furniture. "The fancy fabric usually winds up on the curtains, while the casual fabric goes on the furniture," he says. "I put formality in the items that people don't come into contact with, and use linen velvet, linen damask or inexpensive chintz on the items that people use. The curtains are often made of lined silk."

Salvator prefers curtains with an elaborate, old world quality, replete with all the trimmings. "A room will never look antique without proper curtains," he says. "And so few designers today know how to make them. I learned how to make elegant curtains from one of the best in the business—Mario Buatta. His curtains are beautiful and lush and perfectly draped."

Salvator often garners praise for his curtains, which are favorarbly compared to antique couture ball gowns. Like the rooms they adorn, these drapes are fashionable, finely styled and richly detailed—perfectly suited for a "Prince Somebody."

These Chinese Chippendale-style bamboo chairs and mirrored panels take the edge off of this formal dining room. The novel choice to place electrified candlesticks on the table lends an unexpected antique element to the table.

# WINDOW TREATMENTS

1.

2.

3.

**DESIGNER TIPS: DESIGNING TRADITIONAL CURTAINS BY SCOTT SALVATOR** 1, 2

When it comes to curtains, you have to find a good workroom or seamstress. Almost anyone who can sew can produce attractive curtain panels, but it takes skill to create beautiful valances. The fabric should be cut like fashion, on the bias, so ask to see samples from the person who will produce yours. With a stone or bell valance, for example, the bells must be cut on the bias and attached between the swags. The valance might look like it is all of one piece, but if it's actually made that way, the bells won't form properly. Likewise, if you're making a shaped valance with tails, you have to limit the amount of fabric in the middle, and keep the tails shirred, not pleated. Too much fabric in the middle looks heavy, and pleated tails, like jabots, appear too stiff and flat.

Curtain panels should be interlined with bump flannel. Lining makes curtains look luxurious, giving them a fuller, lusher appearance. It also gives them a longer life, protecting them from fading by the sun. As far as length goes, panels should break two inches onto the floor, creating a slight puddle.

People generally do not come into contact with curtains, so you don't have to worry about the durability of the fabrics you use. I prefer more glamorous and delicate materials, such as silk taffeta. Silk and silk taffeta have more sheen and body, so they reflect light and hang better. Heavy linen also hangs well, but it has a more casual, textured look. Cotton taffeta is somewhere in the middle—it's heavy and hangs well, but also has a very fine finish. It makes great curtains, because of its body.

If you are not working with a designer, the best thing to do is to bring a picture of the type of curtain you want to the person who will produce it. Be sure to ask about fabrics that achieve the look you want.

**DESIGNER TIPS: UPDATED WINDOW TREATMENTS BY CARL D'AQUINO** 3

Curtains and window treatments add softness to a room in a way that only fabric can. A simple sheer, for example, can take the edge off of windows and other architectural details, allowing light to gently filter in. This makes a room look more "finished."

If you're designing in a particular style, window treatments can also add a period note. At our firm, we strive to make every detail of a home reflect the period that inspired it, but we update and simplify windows to reflect a more modern sensibility. Our goal is to create a fresh take on a familiar style—not to have curtains that look like they belong in museums.

In fine 18th-century European and American homes, window treatments were rather elaborate. Popular styles included swags with jabots and long cascading swags over balloon shades. These were frequently made from silk fabrics, complete with trim. We design a cleaner, more tailored version of the original: Instead of silk, we use wool damask, muslin or cotton, and we hang the curtains on a contemporary-looking rod—perhaps one made from Lucite and suspended by satin nickel brackets. It looks classic, but is updated by the restraint shown in the curtain's design, its use of simple fabric and its reliance on modern hardware.

When we're designing for a room with a low ceiling, we'll often stretch curtains from the top of the wall to the bottom, which makes the room look bigger. (It can also accentuate height in larger rooms.) A similar trick works in suburban developments, where window proportions are commonly out of sync with the rest of the room. There we ignore the windows' boundaries and treat the entire wall as a single entity, installing a full-width sheer. If the home has a cheap window trim, mounting a sheer Roman shade will help improve it by masking the details. Light penetrates sheers, but they are perfect for hiding the awkward, unattractive aspects of a generic builder's home.

The key to designing for windows is to remember that they are part of an entire room, and can't be done in isolation. Window treatments must work with all of the other elements in a space and be compatible with their style. In a traditional home, it doesn't matter if the windows are updated or treated historically, so long as they retain a sense of classicism.

**COMPANY IN FOCUS: THE SILK TRADING CO.** 4, 5

It's rare to find a retail shop that sells designer-quality prefabricated curtain panels, which may be why The Silk Trading Co. has been so successful in the 11 years since it was founded. Customers like instant gratification, say company founders Warren and Andrea Kay, who also cite their product's high quality and accessibility as reasons for its popularity. Winner of *Elle Decor*'s 2003 Design Award for fabrics, The Silk Trading Co. makes purchases easy: Simply visit a showroom, pick from a selection of fabrics, give the salesperson your measurements and let them consult their stock. If necessary, you can borrow memos or swatches to preview the fabrics' colors in your home before purchasing—a wise decision, as you are not allowed to return prefabricated curtains. This "drapery out-of-a-box" also comes in velvet, chenille, Egyptian cotton, and linen, and can be lined and interlined with cotton, in a variety of lengths. The company will measure your windows and install the curtains, and panels can be easily hemmed to suit your needs. As the company's product line and services expand each year, its reputation also grows: At present, it offers panels, custom drapes and upholstery and sells fabric by the yard. Consult its website for 22 showroom locations, to order memos, swatches and curtains, or to contact a design consultant. Retail. **Call 800-854-0396 or visit www.silktrading.com.**

4.

5.

**COMPANY IN FOCUS: THE CURTAIN EXCHANGE** 6

At the Curtain Exchange, customers are allowed to take full-length curtains home, try them out, and then return what doesn't work. It's a huge selling point, and an option unavailable from most other retailers and workrooms. "We help our customers buy with confidence," says company founder Georgina O'Hara Callan, a former interior designer. Curtain Exchange offers treatments made from silk, linen, chenille, cotton and a host of other materials, often with beautiful embroidery or in patterns such as toile and damask. Its highly fashionable inventory is always changing. "We make limited quantities of each style," Callan explains. "As a result, the curtains you buy are fairly exclusive. We do this to offer variety and to keep the product unique—we don't want our customers to walk into their neighbors' home and see the same curtains." The company's website puts shoppers in touch with a design consultant, shows them how to measure windows, and provides contact information for ordering. By the end of 2004, there will be over 20 Curtain Exchange showrooms in the U.S. Retail. **Call 504-897-2444 or visit www.thecurtainexchange.com.**

6.

*Most people generally buy window treatments from regional sources. Designers have their favorite workrooms, but if you don't have a designer, referrals are the best way to go. (In addition to fabric treatments, most workrooms also make blinds and interior shutters, which can be custom-painted or stained to match your décor.) The following sources sell designer-quality treatments and related products on the Internet and at retail outlets and showrooms around the country.*

## SHUTTERS, VENETIAN BLINDS, & SHADES

### HARTMANN & FORBES

Portland, OR-based Hartmann & Forbes uses age-old Japanese techniques to make finely hand-woven Roman shades, curtains and cornices from organic materials such as bark, bamboo, linen and husk. The company's curtains are defined by their old world appeal, but the simple variety and organic materials also make them appropriate for more contemporary settings. Hartmann & Forbes has 15 showrooms across the U.S., including one in Hawaii. To the Trade. **Call 888-582-8780 or visit www.hfshades.com.**

### HORIZON SHUTTERS 1, 2

Horizon Shutters has been turning out customized, handmade and hand-finished shutters for over 25 years. Seven years ago, it also became the first U.S. company to sell such pieces online. Run by father-and-son team Jack and Brian Wright, Horizon makes high-quality traditional and plantation shutters from solid basswood, which is known for its resistance to warping. Basic stained versions come in 10 different colors, which are dipped, rubbed, sealed, sanded and protected with two topcoats. Painted shutters come in 13 colors and are sealed, sanded, primed, re-sanded and finished with two satin-finish topcoats. Shutters are available in finished and unfinished versions; stains and colors can be customized. The company's website offers highly detailed measuring instructions. Retail. **Call 888-399-4947 or visit www.horizonshutters.com.**

### HUNTER DOUGLAS

A familiar name in window treatments, Hunter Douglas has been selling shades, blinds and shutters for over 50 years. Its products come finished in a set selection of colors and stains, with its wooden blinds and shutters being the most historically styled. Sheer shades are also available. The company's website lists local dealers; look for those that offer measurement and installation services. Retail. **Call 800-937-STYLE or visit www.hunterdouglas.com.**

## WINDOW TREATMENT HARDWARE

### JOSEPH BIUNNO 3, 4

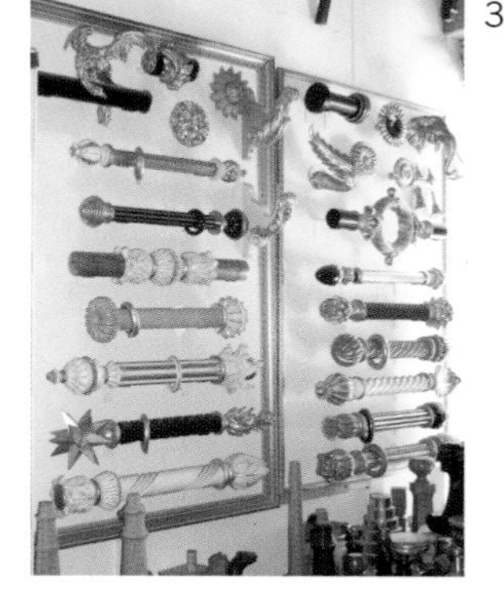

3.

4.

When designers need traditional wooden hardware for their window treatments, they head straight for Joseph Biunno. With over 35 years' experience hand-carving furniture and restoring antiques, Biunno is well-known in the industry. He began his career at his father's small, yet well-respected, restoration shop, where clients included top-tier firms McMillan and Parish-Hadley. Biunno has kept such longtime clients and added impressive new ones, expanding the business to include window treatment hardware, furniture reproductions and replacement locks and keys. He now has over 200 historically inspired finial and tieback designs, which can either be hand-carved or, more affordably, cast in resin. (The finial poles come in about 20 different styles and are made from poplar wood, unless otherwise specified.) Biunno's hardware is on view at eight U.S. showrooms, and is available in hand-painted, hand-finished and unfinished versions. Retail and To the Trade. **Call 212-629-5630 or visit www.antiquefurnitureusa.com.**

### DESIRON

When they founded Desiron (in 1997), brothers Frank and Matthew Carfaro were carrying on a family tradition established by their great-grandfather, who was an ironsmith in Italy.

1.

2.

Designers love the company's metal window treatment hardware and custom services, which have just become available to retail shoppers. But Desiron also offers contemporary furniture and accessories, and prefabricated hardware for window treatments, sold through a home design website (www.homeportfolio.com) and at its Manhattan showroom. Retail and To the Trade. **Call 212-353-2600 or visit www.desiron.com.**

**FINIALS BY JOHN RAGSDALE** 5, 6

Finials by John Ragsdale has been selling decorative wooden curtain hardware—poles, finials, rings, wall brackets, tiebacks and cord pulls—for the last 25 years. Available in finished and unfinished versions, all products can be custom-painted by company artists to match clients' fabrics and walls; standard finishes include gold leaf, silver leaf, and mahogany. The company's Egg series is truly beautiful, a tribute to Russia's colorful Easter eggs. Its Animal series includes leopard and cheetah finials, which add a hint of whimsical chic to rooms. Decorative lamp finials and coronas (bed crowns used to create wall canopies) are also available. Retail. **Call 843-766-4114 or visit www.ragsdalefinials.com.**

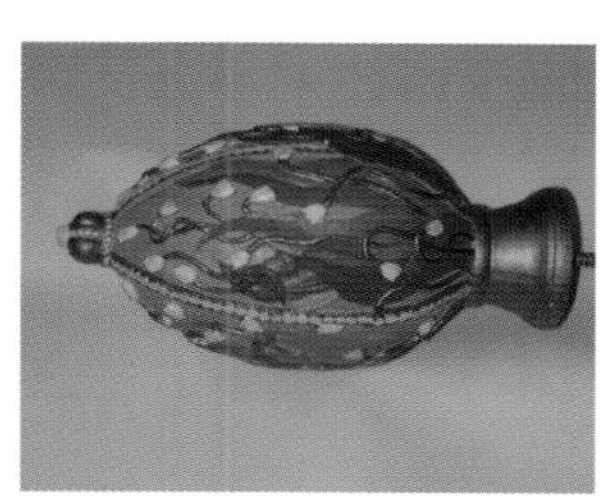
5.

6.

## TRIM

**M&J TRIMMING** 7, 8

In its own subtle way, trim ties together all of the colors in a room, adding another layer of refinement to it. Every imaginable type of decorative interior trim is on view at fashion-industry favorite M&J Trimming—from leather cords to velvet jacquards and mohair fringe. Interior designer Elissa Cullman compares its Manhattan showroom to a candy store. Retail. **Call 212-842-5050 or visit www.mjtrim.com.**

7.

**SAMUEL & SONS**

Geared to high-end residential and commercial interiors, this trade-only division of M&J Trimming offers a wide range of products, from traditional silk tassel fringes to contemporary leather piping. Most trimmings are imported from Europe, but the company sources "the entire world," with pieces coming from as far away as Africa. (Reflecting its international bent, Samuel & Sons refers to trim as "passementerie," the French translation of its name.) Though it opened a mere five years ago, S & S already carries 20,000 trimmings and is represented in 11 showrooms in major cities across the country. The New York showroom carries all of their stock, which is available for overnight delivery. To the Trade. **Call 212-704-8000 or visit www.samuelandsons.com.**

**CLARENCE HOUSE** 9, 10

Clarence House carries a full line of trimmings in silk, cotton, linen and wool. Many of its styles are based on archival documents, which detail the trimming found in the châteaus of Fontainebleau and Versailles. The company sells both simple and elaborate pieces; highlights include bouillon fringe and key tassels, while a new French coral tieback, made from wire and silk, duplicates that creature's beautiful, tangled branches. See the section on textiles for more information on this source. To the Trade. **Call 800-221-4704 or visit www.clarencehouse.com.**

8.

9.

10.
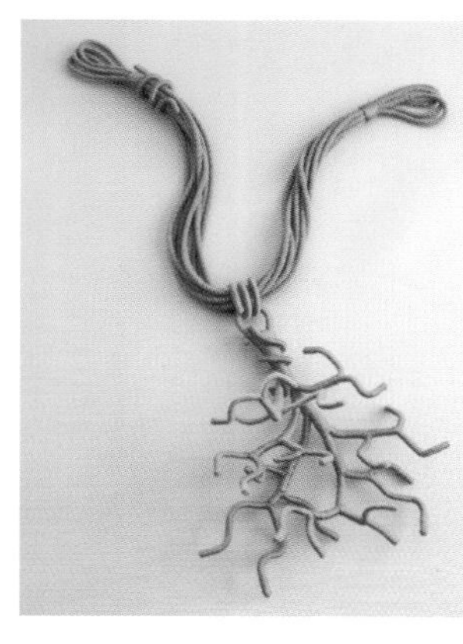

ROBERT COUTURIER

CHAPTER 7

# GRAND EUROPEAN STYLE

Not many interior designers can say they built a palace, but Robert Couturier can. He has not only built one, but has rehabilitated two others for one particularly wealthy client. In fact, palaces are old hat for Couturier—he's lived in them before. Today he is one of the few designers who can tackle projects of such magnitude with grace and subtlety.

Born into a prominent French family, Couturier grew up in a hotel particulier in Paris' 16th arrondissement that was designed by renowned architect Hector Guimard and interior designer Jean-Michel Frank. As a boy, Couturier played architect with Legos within those well-appointed walls, as well as in the confines of his family's countryside castles. After attending Paris' école Camondo and traveling widely to study architecture, he moved to Manhattan, where he has been designing new spaces in his distinct version of old world elegance ever since.

The rooms pictured in this chapter illustrate Couturier's range, including both a European-inspired Manhattan apartment and an unpretentious Connecticut country home. The designer has a simple recipe for creating an antique-inspired space: Keep the rooms traditional and the design orderly, and fill it with a diverse mix of antique furniture, architectural details, interesting textiles, rugs and wallpaper and artisan-applied wall finishes.

It is his brand of eclecticism, in fact, that defines his high-minded and worldly design style. "Eclectic is the European way of designing," Couturier says. "People inherit pieces and keep them because they are from their families. As a result, their rooms are much more eclectic by nature than most American rooms. Their contents provide variety and extraordinary conversation."

Couturier's rooms reveal his desire to give his rooms a broad sense of design history, as well as his

**Opposite:** Antique carved wooden doors from a 17th-century Spanish castle now adorn this gutted and rebuilt Manhattan apartment. Their carvings delicately balance the flower-like shapes of the chandelier, which was made in Murano, Italy.

affection for French design—especially for 18th- and early 20th-century styles. "I prefer French 18th-century design because in my opinion it was the period of the highest form of decorative arts ever achieved," he says. "Every detail was cared for, which created extraordinary shapes and forms and a great sense of luxury. And I love French furniture from the 1940s—it's elegant and simple and can be mixed with everything."

Couturier's work is perhaps most inspired by two 18th-century French design periods: the rococo and the neoclassical. The former was a more restrained outgrowth of the exaggerated, lavish and curvaceous forms of the Baroque, and was marked by furniture that retains a sense of disorderliness in its sinuous and asymmetrical forms. The neoclassic period that followed was largely inspired by the excavations of the Italian cities of Pompeii and Herculaneum, which renewed interest in the designs of ancient Greece and Rome.

Couturier's pied-à-terre is wildly eclectic. The pedigreed antiques and custom-painted walls contrast with the simple architectural shell, creating positive visual tension between the many forms and materials.

Like Couturier, many of today's designers are inspired by the furniture and interior design of the 1940s, including the work of Jean-Michael Frank. This is due, in part, to the simple, modern forms of that era. In particular, French designers of the forties achieved a balance between the traditional elements of the earlier periods and the sleek lines of modernism. Their designs serve as an aesthetic bridge, linking past and present.

## The Eclectic Pied-à-Terre

Located in a two-story converted SoHo loft, Couturier's Manhattan pied-à-terre and office space are a strong reflection of his design style. To suit the sensibilities of a loft space, Couturier kept the architectural detailing to a minimum and used his collection of valuable antiques to distinguish the rooms. The living area—which doubles as his sleeping quarters— is filled with eclectic items that boast a wide range of pedigree and history. Couturier placed a curvaceous Louis XV

DESIGNER TIPS

**Blend Styles:** European families tend to hand down furniture through the generations, giving their homes an eclectic look. To create an old world style in your home, mix antiques and reproductions from a broad range of design periods and countries.

**Use Bold Color Palettes:** Traditionally, Europeans embrace strong colors, which can make the largest rooms feel cozy. Choose complex color schemes that add richness and sophistication to rooms.

**Consider French Styles:** 18th-century French design is considered one of the great eras of design. For a high-style look in your home, think about adding reproductions from this period. Also consider French 1940s design. Due to its simple yet elegant forms, it complements most other styles—it is appreciated and widely imitated today.

**Start Simple:** Use symmetrical architectural details to give rooms a sense of order and tradition when filling them with eclectic collections of furniture and artifacts.

daybed next to a square Egyptian throne, across from two rounded glass chairs that were on display at the 1936 Paris Arts Decortifs Exposition. The room also features two stools designed by legendary designer Elsie de Wolfe, an authentic Louis XV armchair and two 18th-century Chinese bookcases.

"When I design a room, I like to think about the people who lived with the antiques I choose," Couturier says. "I imagine them all sitting around having a conversation—and then the room becomes alive and truly fascinating to me. In my pied-à-terre, it would be quite a cocktail party."

For Couturier, the more wildly eclectic the design, the better. "I'm flamboyant," he explains. "Like most Europeans, I'm not afraid of color. I embrace it. I sleep on a daybed upholstered in bright pink vintage silk. For me, it could not be dressed in any other color." (Of course, luxury has a price: The daybed cost $80,000.)

Because he loves flamboyant, feminine forms and eclectic arrangements, Couturier creates architectural shells that provide a stable foundation for what he calls "every possible craziness." "I like rooms that are well-organized in their layout and architecture," says Couturier. "There has to be balance and simplicity to the architecture. It creates a tight geometric structure—and then, you can put anything you want in the room."

## The Eclectic Country Home

The four-year-old neoclassical-inspired Connecticut home that Couturier built and shares with his partner, Jeffrey Morgan, is quite different from his Manhattan apartment. Strong architectural details and a symmetrical, orderly framework lend this early Connecticut country house an air of high European style. And unlike his pied-à-terre, the antiques that fill these rooms are more finishing touches that round out an

In Couturier's country home, Delft urns sit atop an 18th-century Florentine stone mantel. The rococo fire screen's curved lines nicely contrast with the mantel's square shape.

The large 18th-century French mantel, made from limestone, creates a strong focal point in the living room. Its restrained glamour blends nicely with the eclectic furniture arrangement, including the straight lines of the sofa designed by Couturier.

The restrained neoclassical architectural details, seen in the ceiling beams and wall moldings, help unify this small library. A niche was added to create an intimate reading spot, then lined with fabric to soften and warm the space.

authentic 19th-century setting.

While carefully chosen moldings, paneling, antiques and salvaged architectural elements contribute to its old world charm, Couturier feels that the home's 3,000-square-foot scale is what truly anchors it in the past. "People build huge homes that look like the original versions on steroids, and then don't use half the space," he laments. "And they frequently run out of money trying to decorate them. The scale of this

Vintage Fortuny fabric stretches across a long foyer wall, creating a focal point. The 18th-century Italian mirror, originally a clock, adds a touch of whimsy, while a simple 19th-century oak table adds an unpretentious note.

*"I like to add rich* ***texture*** *to walls where there is not much interest... Unlike with wallpaper,* ***artisans*** *can achieve the perfect scale, shape and color to* ***personalize*** *walls."*

house allows the rooms to be comfortable and inviting."

## Authentic Old World Design

Couturier's other work is a varied mix for a diverse clientele, and he tries to be selective about which projects to take on. He is not the architect to go to if you're looking for the latest in great room design. Rather, Couturier looks for clients who value his encyclopedic knowledge of old world style, as well as his ability to transform a generic, new home into a fashionable, and seemingly generations-old, European one.

While his main design approach is to use eclectic furniture set within traditional architectural shells, as his own residences demonstrate, Couturier is also known for using salvaged architectural details, custom wall treatments, and vintage textiles, wallpapers and rugs to achieve the appearance of old world design. "I seldom use copies of anything, with the exception of light fixtures," he says. "The real thing seems more honest."

A mix of worldly choices lies at the heart of all of Couturier's designs. In a palace he built in Mexico, Couturier installed a wall from an Indian palace in the living room, scattered sculptures from the Far East throughout the home and enriched the dining room with a collection of decorative plaques from a French hotel particulier. Similarly, in one Manhattan apartment, he installed a large 18th-century limestone fireplace he'd found in Paris, as well as a pair of antique doors from a dismantled Spanish castle.

To seamlessly blend salvaged architectural pieces into newly built rooms, Couturier uses old world building techniques and clever design decisions. In the Manhattan apartment, that meant placing the mantlepiece from Paris atop a jamb made of briquettes—slivers of brick cobbled together in an ancient French masonry method. Couturier also matched the wood tone of the Spanish doors with the reclaimed wooden floors that ran beneath them, creating a subtle alliance between the classic materials and the newly built space.

Generally, Couturier's walls are richly patterned, frequently in complementary tone-on-tone colors. He hires decorative artists (including his favorite, Baulin Paris) to apply

This dining room doubles as a library, lending it an additional layer of character. For an authentic, lived-in feel, the shelves are lined with everyday books, rather than a collection of leather-bound books. The light fixtures were made from vintage Christmas decorations once on display at Macy's.

DESIGNER TIPS

**Build to Scale:** When building a period-inspired home, build it to the scale of the original style. If you don't want low ceiling heights and small windows, don't update a standard Colonial, as the raised ceiling heights will create awkward exterior proportions. Instead, chose an antique style with more suitable proportions. Look at some of the neoclassical models, such as Federal or Greek Revival.

**Use Antique Elements:** Vintage architectural details, textiles, rugs and fabrics are an excellent way to give a space old world charm.

**Consider Custom Wall Treatments:** Custom wall treatments add richness and personalize spaces. They make all of the elements in a room look more attractive, especially artwork on display.

**Match Building Methods with Details:** When incorporating salvaged architectural details, use old world building methods, including masonry techniques, to properly incorporate the older elements into a new space. Use complementary salvaged elements, such as doors and flooring, and complementary wood tones, to create a cohesive look.

**Seek Out Antique Wallpaper and Textiles:** Antique wallpaper, such as Zuber, and textiles, such as Fortuny, add unrivaled richness to rooms. If the originals are unavailable or impractical, look for good reproductions.

Couturier uses a variety of patterns and furniture styles in his rooms to create truly eclectic spaces. They are successful because of the balance created by the neoclassic architectural details and strictly ordered furniture arrangements.

designs, inspired by large fabric patterns, to the walls. "I like to add texture to walls where there is not much interest," he says. "It adds to the layered look I like to achieve. Unlike with wallpaper, artisans can achieve the perfect scale, shape and color to personalize walls."

Couturier says that these rich treatments make everything in a room look better—especially artwork. "Custom painting enriches rooms in a strong way," he says. "And it makes art look twice as good."

When it comes to wallpaper, Couturier prefers Zuber, which was originally produced in 19th-century Europe and is still considered among the world's finest. Famed for its stunning panoramic trompe l'oeil landscapes, the paper was made using thousands of hand-carved blocks and hundreds of colors. As for vintage textiles, Couturier feels there's no equal to the work of late Spanish fabric designer Mariano Fortuny.

Taken as a whole, Couturier's European aesthetic and the work of his talented artisans transforms new spaces into seemingly antique, character-rich rooms. The neoclassical architectural details and symmetrical furniture arrangements he favors provide an ordered framework for collections of pedigreed, eclectic antiques. But perhaps more than anything else, it is the timelessness of his designs that make them so successful. Highly fashionable, yet deeply comfortable, Couturier's rooms look as if they had developed over generations. They look, in fact, as through they had always been there.

Four rooms radiate from this circular entrance hall, which features large moldings that were added to give the space a sense of architecture. The star on the ceiling is repeated on the floor, playfully giving direction while creating visual interest. Deep-set bookshelves, upholstered benches and custom-painted walls give the space a sense of warmth.

# TEXTILES

## DESIGNER TIPS: FABRICS FOR TRADITIONAL HOMES BY ELISSA CULLMAN 1, 2

If you've already selected historic-looking architecture, hardware and woodwork for your home, the next step is finding matching textiles. This is quite easy: Many showrooms have fabric archives or designs based on significant textiles from museums and older homes. In-house designers can often alter the scale, pattern and colors to create updated versions of these designs. Ask a salesperson to guide you to fabrics that suit your home's look and the style of your furniture, which are appropriate for the way you live.

1.

2.

If you want your upholstery to look antique, find the original patterns. Most 18th-century Sheraton-style furniture should be upholstered in striped or small-scale woven fabrics; 19th-century Arts and Crafts furniture should be upholstered in leather or, again, a smaller woven textile. For these pieces, large-scale damasks and multicolored checks would be inappropriate, even though they are traditional in style. It's better to find an updated reinterpretation of a historic design.

When conducting your search for the right textile, you may find that older design materials don't suit contemporary lifestyles. For example, a traditional silk fabric may have looked lovely in an 18th-century drawing room, yet be too delicate for your living area. But if you like the way it looks, ask showrooms if they can work with you to change the construction of the ground material.

## DESIGNER TIPS: GREAT UPHOLSTERED PIECES BY SCOTT SALVATOR 3, 4

Two things make great upholstery: quality and design.

For truly durable upholstered furniture, start with a kiln-dried, maple wood frame. Look for one with no knots, which can weaken the furniture and cause it to break over time. Make sure that the joints are doweled and glued (the fewer joints, the better), and that braces are added.

3.

The kind of spring you choose is determined by the type of furniture you're dealing with. The springs you use for a seat will naturally be heavier than those that support someone's back. Firm springs are very important when you're working on a dining banquette, or any chair or sofa with a "tight" seat, as they have to be strong enough to hold a person's weight. Tie the springs to the webbing with strong, waxed Italian twine.

And if you use seat cushions, fill them with 100 percent white European goose down—the purest and softest—and add two layers of ticking.

When I design upholstered furniture, I do so with the client's size and build in mind. In general, a deeper inside seat of about 24 to 26 inches is most comfortable. A pillow can always be added if it is too short. Plan on a width of about 30 to 33 inches for each person—more than 33 inches will throw off the scale (unless the client is very overweight).

Woven fabrics make for practical and attractive upholstery. Some curtain fabrics can also be used as upholstery, provided they have a backing and do not get a lot of use. If the fabric has a loose weave, like chenille, it will have to be backed. I prefer acrylic backing to fabric—acrylic is stronger, more flexible, and lasts longer. Blended fabrics are also strong, and cotton-and-synthetic materials just wear better. Have all upholstered pieces stain-protected.

4.

**ARTISANS: ROLLINS & ISLES, PINTURA** 5

Pintura founders Ed Rollins and Chris Isles specialize in hand-printed fabrics that update traditional European and Asian designs. "We mine decorative art history, then give it a contemporary look," Rollins explains from their Manhattan studio. Pintura designs are based on the duo's research into textiles at the New York Public Library, as well as on the decorative motifs they see when traveling abroad. Known for their artisanal quality, the fabrics appear to be hand-stenciled, but are in fact (more cost-effectively) hand-screened. Pintura also produces custom fabrics, including hand-painted versions for private clients and design firms such as Cullman & Kravis and MAC II. A line of silk fabrics is available through A.M. Collections. To the Trade. **Call 212-995-8655.**

5.

**ARTISANS: KAZUMI YOSHIDA, CLARENCE HOUSE** 6

When Kazumi Yoshida was a young man, he drew sketches for fashion designer Mary McFadden. His work soon caught the eye of Clarence House founder Robin Roberts, who immediately hired the talented artist. For the past 22 years, Yoshida has been the company's design director, turning out work that garners raves for its beauty and originality. Designers say his interpretations of antique textiles are as masterly and inventive as his newer creations—and indeed, Yoshida finds inspiration everywhere, from ballets and menus to archival docu-

6.

ments. Recent creations include Nouveau Bizarre, a stylized silk lampas floral based on a 17th-century motif; Fujiwara, a woven linen inspired by an archival document of Chinese costumes; and Jembala, a wool crewel influenced by an 18th-century Indian tree of life pattern. "I didn't come to textile design by the usual route, and I don't follow trends," Yoshida explains. "I fell into this work, which I think is a good thing. I bring an outside perspective, which allows me to create something unique." To the Trade. **Call 800-803-2850 or visit www.clarencehouse.com.**

*In addition to the aforementioned sources, the following companies are interior designers' favorite sources for antique textiles and traditional patterns, many of which also produce fashionably updated designs based on archival documents. It's always best to examine and touch fabrics before you purchase them; contact showrooms or check out a company's website to find a list of local retailers.*

**A.M. COLLECTIONS** 1
Anthony Mott started his business five years ago, after working as an executive for top-shelf textile companies such as Christopher Hyland and Rogers & Goffigan. He now represents a group of U.S. artisans who use old-world techniques to create intriguing new textiles. All of their fabrics are hand-printed, hand-blocked or handwoven; most reinterpret ancient motifs or rely on novel materials. "Our company aims to give designers exactly what they want," Mott explains from his Manhattan studio. "They can request specific color and fabrics. They don't have to buy tired-looking patterns." Interior designers Elissa Cullman and Robert Couturier shop at A.M. Collections; one of Mott's artisans, Lucretia Moroni, is also a well-known interiors expert. Trained as a trompe l'oeil painter in Italy, her fabrics tend to be inspired by Venetian designs, which she reinterprets in exuberant, unusual colors. Custom carpets are also available. For more on Moroni's work, see the flooring section. To the Trade. **Call 212-625-2616.**

**OLD WORLD WEAVERS**
As its name suggests, Old World Weavers produces textiles based on vintage patterns. Its silk taffeta Frullino broche, which references 18th-century embroidery, was inspired by a document found at the Louvre's prestigious Musée des Arts Decoratifs. In a tribute to the rich fabrics of the Renaissance, Old World Weavers produces 35 patterns, circa 16th century, which use large-scale damasks (such as Mattais) and small geometric motifs (such as Diam) that have been hand-screened and -painted on cotton for a pointedly antique look. The company also provides a fresh take on traditional designs, as in its Giardino collection, which updates vintage patterns with unusual materials. One example of this intriguing approach: A stylized Indian motif and damask pattern on contemporary grass cloth. Old World Weavers is owned by Stark. To the Trade. **Call 212-355-7186 or visit www.old-world-weavers.com**

**BRUNSCHWIG & FILS** 2
Established in 1900, Brunschwig & Fils has a strong sense of tradition. The textile company rarely retires its designs. As a result, many patterns date back over 50 years—and some pre-date the company. A hand-woven Louis XV ecru silk brocade is made in the same French atelier that wove fabrics for the restoration of the Chateau de Versailles, while brocades, lampas and velvets created for Louis XIV are produced today on the very same looms as the originals in their 18th predecessors. Other notable textiles include the rich Mariah Crewel Embroidery which is hand sewn and its intricate Barnstable Chenille Damask textiles which use a fresh material to reinterpret traditional designs. To the Trade. **Call 212- 838-7878 or visit www.brunschwigfils.com.**

**KIME**
With a client list that includes the Prince of Wales and Lord Lloyd Webber, Robert Kime is one of England's best-known designers. His antique-inspired fabrics are considered some of the finest traditional textiles available; all are hand-printed or handwoven, and range from faded linens with Arts and Crafts motifs to vibrant, intricate chinoiserie patterns. To the Trade, through John Rosselli. **Call 212-593-2060 or visit www.robertkime.co.uk.**

**CORA GINSBURG**
Designers have been going to Cora Ginsburg for antique textiles since 1973. One of America's top antique fabric dealers, Ginsburg originally sold to U.S. museums and European institutions, but her Manhattan-based gallery now offers its wares to the public, with high-end textiles that include embroidery, woven silks and printed cottons dating back to the 17th century. The gallery's current owner, Titi Halle, has owned it for eight years, and offers consultation and appraisal services. Retail. **Call 212-744-1352 or visit www.coraginsburg.com.**

**SCHUMACHER** 3

Founded over a century ago, Schumacher first gained fame as an importer of European decorative fabrics, dressing some of the finest homes in America, including the White House. (Its colorful silk brocade, dubbed White House Lampas, was used for the curtains in the State Dining Room.) These days, the company turns out historical reproductions and imaginative new patterns, including a line of botanical fabrics designed by acclaimed muralist Chuck Fischer. These finely engraved, hand-printed fabrics, which bear names like Chinese Pavilion and Palm Trellis, capture the unique character of Fischer's decorative work. (For a look at the artist's murals and to learn more about his work, turn to the section on walls and chapter 6, *Twisted Traditional*.) To the Trade. **Call 212-415-3900 or visit www.fschumacher.com**

1.

**SILK SURPLUS**

Located in an elegantly designed Manhattan townhouse, just steps from Manhattan's D&D building (where many of New York's finest "to the trade" showrooms are located), Silk Surplus is the only place to go for deep discounts on Scalamandre textiles. Prices are up to 80 percent off retail, which makes the store a favorite with designers: According to the owner, they comprise almost half his business. Silk Surplus also carries its own line of attractive Baranzelli fabrics. Retail. **Call 212-753-6511.**

**MAISON DÉCOR**

Maison Décor, a retail textile and interior design company, was founded in Spain over a decade ago. It is part of a larger textile company, Intextil, which has been in existence for 35 years and is noted for producing Pepe Peñalver fabrics (available only to the trade). But with more than 50 locations abroad and a U.S. outlet in Greenwich, CT, Maison Décor definitely stands on its own. Its beautiful, traditionally designed fabrics are made at some of the best textile mills in the world, and include gorgeous pieces such as Catenia, a stylized, classic-looking cotton floral, and Country, a printed toile reminiscent of 17th-century patterns. The company's detailed, user-friendly website allows you to preview textiles; the store can provide actual samples. Retail. **Call 203-422-0440 or visit www.maisondecor.info.**

2.

3.

TONY INGRAO

CHAPTER 8

# GEORGIAN REDEFINED

From the very outset of his career, Tony Ingrao has possessed an exceptional talent for designing new spaces in an old world style. After graduating from the Rhode Island School of Design nearly 25 years ago, he was charged with the creation of a sumptuous, Louis XIV palace. The project took seven years to complete, but the end result rivaled the opulence of Versailles. And although much of his work is inspired by one historic style, such as Georgian or Gothic, his spaces are never airless, stiff period rooms. Rather, they are fresh, lively and full of light.

Ingrao's clients range from society figures to celebrities like Kim Cattrall and Goldie Hawn. He designed the two homes featured here—a permanent residence and a beach house—for one prominent family. The more formal main house is perched just steps from the Long Island Sound, while the Long Island beach house serves as the family's summer home. Both were built from scratch with the help of famed architect Francis Fleetwood.

"Every client has a vision of what their home should be," Ingrao says. "We create their fantasy."

For the Long Island main house, creating the clients' fantasy meant that the team would be constructing a 19th-century Shingle style exterior and an 18th-century Georgian era interior. The beach house would also have a Shingle style exterior, but its interior would be classic Americana. Shingle style homes were popularized by famed architecture firm McKim, Mead and White, who designed them with large rooms and tall ceilings. Amply and expertly proportioned, these homes are well suited to the needs of contemporary life.

**Opposite:** The main foyer (seen here beyond the living room) has a double-height ceiling, which is tempered by a grand stairwell that Ingrao modeled after one he spied in an 18th-century Southern home. Rich architectural details, including pilasters and crown moldings, break up the expanse of the first floor walls.

Fleetwood chose historic materials for the exterior of the main house, using Connecticut fieldstone for its masonry base, red cedar for its shingles and slate tiles for its roof. The low-slung roofline, punctuated with gables and terraces, gave the architecture its signature Shingle style look. The design of the windows is the one area where the home departs from traditional Shingle style elements: To bring additional light into the interiors, the clients requested a greater number of windows and larger openings than found in traditional Shingle style homes.

This formal dining room's main attraction is the Long Island Sound, which can be seen through the large windows. To balance the great expanse, Ingrao added rich 18th-century chinoiserie wallpaper with three-dimensional details. This also added warmth and appeared to enlarge the room.

## The Interior Challenge

In the interior spaces, the clients wanted a traditional, well-appointed environment. Ingrao's challenge was to design an antique-filled space that would still be appropriate for children. Other challenges included modulating the scale of the large rooms, which were 12 feet tall at minimum.

Ingrao chose a mid-to-late Georgian style for the interior. England's Georgian era stretched from the early 1700s to the early 1800s, and encompassed a number of

*"To* **balance** *the Sound's great* **expanse,** *I introduced an 18th-century* **wall covering** *from China, which gave the space* **warmth** *and made it seem larger."*

design movements, including Rococo, Palladian and neoclassical. The particular period Ingrao used for the house was dominated by furniture designers such as Robert Adams, Thomas Chippendale, George Hepplewhite and Thomas Sheraton, all of whom were influenced by classic Greek and Roman design.

The first step was to soften these classic styles and give them a fresh, contemporary sensibility. "Our goal was to create a classically designed environment that wasn't off-putting or stuffy," explains Ingrao, who designed the home with colleague Randy Kemper. "We wanted to update Georgian style and give it a more youthful appearance."

To achieve this younger look, Ingrao chose a pale, reclaimed antique English oak for the home's floors. He then flew in floor polishers from France, who added a deep, layered patina to the wood. Seams, grain and knots make the floor look respectfully worn, as though it had existed in the home for decades. The weathered flooring counterbalanced the home's fine antiques furniture and Persian rugs, lending them a more informal air. "The flooring softened the space," Ingrao remembers. "Stone would have made it cold, and dark wood would have made it too formal."

To create a sense of intimacy and history in the larger rooms, Ingrao selected strong architectural details, complex color schemes, rich textiles and antique furniture, rugs and light fixtures. Interesting artwork and antique decorative accessories helped add the final touch.

**Above, left:** Antique English oak floors lend this traditionally designed living room a refreshing, youthful informality. If the flooring had been stained the tone of the room's English antiques, it would have more closely resembled a Georgian period room.

**Above, right:** In this boy's bedroom, an antique library step leads up to a tall, four-poster bed. A whimsical folk art painting of a military scene adds a charming, masculine touch.

To temper the scale of this foyer, a large light fixture was suspended from the ceiling. A low-backed chair, located beneath a window, reveals the passageway's true size.

DESIGNER TIPS

**Mix Historic Styles:** When designing a new home in a traditional way, combine historic looks. Try mixing a 19th-century Shingle style exterior and an 18th-century Georgian-inspired interior.

**Build with Rescued Architectural Details:** Architectural salvage, including floorboards, enrich new spaces in the same way that antique furniture, carpeting and accessories do. Think of it as a perk for a newly old home.

**Make it Proportional:** Light fixtures are essential to disguising the size of double-height ceilings. Large versions excite the eye and modulate the scale of towering ceilings or other oversized elements, such as tall windows and grand staircases.

**Modernize Window Design:** Update a historic house style by increasing the size and number of your home's windows. To do so without ruining the appearance of the home's historically-inspired façade, mimic the period style's windows and simply enlarge them proportionally. Depending on your home's style, you may choose double-hung or leaded windows, either of which will retain an antique flavor. Inside, use architectural details to disguise their height, capping them with small projecting crowns where appropriate.

**Look to Period Homes:** Base the design of structural elements—such as stairwells—on historic models. For inspiration, visit period homes and museums, or consult architecture books.

**Remove the Velvet Rope:** Make antiques child-friendly by upholstering them in cotton and wool instead of more delicate and often expensive fabrics such as silk.

**Focus on Flooring:** A floor makes a huge impact on a room. Wooden floors seem warm, while stone is typically perceived as cold (unless you choose a rustic tile or mosaic pattern). Dark wood floors look formal in traditionally designed rooms, while classic rooms with pale or washed-out wood flooring appear more youthful and informal.

**Choose Oversized Area Rugs:** Place large antique or reproductions rugs in equally large rooms. They anchor spaces and help bring down the scale.

## Architectural Detailing

To add depth to the home's interiors, Ingrao turned to the Georgian architectural details, including the paneling, wainscoting, molding and stairways that adorn many classically designed homes. A stately staircase in the double-height entry hall was modeled after one from an 18th-century Virginia home, while the custom moldings were reproduced from pieces that adorned two well-known structures—the White House, designed by James Hoban, and Thomas Jefferson's Monticello. Items like these add a classic Georgian touch.

Ingrao also used architectural details to disguise the height of the windows by capping them with small projecting crowns. "In some of the rooms, the windows rise almost to the ceilings, which isn't typical of those in historic homes," he explains. "We used the crown to give a sense of depth and weight to them. It allows them to blend seamlessly into the walls."

In addition to the wood flooring, Ingrao installed other architectural salvage in the home, including fireplace mantels and light fixtures. In the dining room, an antique Georgian mantel provided a perfect complement to the 18th-century furniture and chinoiserie wallpaper. "The piece contributed to the period authenticity of the room and added a patina of age," Ingrao recalls.

This beach house foyer, with its rustic cabinet, colorful hooked rug and other antiques, is a good example of the beach house's Americana theme.

## Antiquing It

As the client desired, the home was filled with pedigreed antiques, which added character in a way that few reproductions could. The furniture includes 18th-century George II, George III and Chippendale pieces, as well as 19th-century Chinese items. Ingrao shopped for the furnishings at auctions, and in Paris and London. "The wife's parents were antique dealers," says Ingrao. "She is used to living with them and understands how important antiques are to creating rooms with a history."

To make the antiques as childproof as possible, Ingrao upholstered them in soft, durable materials. "We used cotton and wools—and avoided silks—which kept the environment family-friendly," he explains. The textiles, many of which featured needlepoint and crewelwork, were inspired by Georgian patterns.

Gorgeous antique and reproduction rugs were then placed throughout the house. The dining room recieved a 19th-century Sultanabad carpet, bought at a Christie's auc-

**Above:** Strong architectural details, including an oversized tiled fireplace and crossbeam ceiling, work with large, upholstered furniture to make this beach house living room feel cozy.

**Opposite:** In this spacious beach house's secondary entrance, charming decorative details—nautical light fixtures, folk art, a hooked rug and plaid, upholstered seat cushions—add warmth and character.

DESIGNER TIPS

**For a Beach House, Think Americana:** An Americana theme is charming for a summer home. To add a sense of warmth and history, include rusticated furniture, light fixtures and folk art.

**Let the Outdoors In:** In summer homes, the barriers between indoors and out should be reduced by including large, expansive windows and rooms with wide-paneled doors that open up to balconies and patios.

**Make Great Rooms Practical:** Your home may be based on a historic model, but it's always a good idea to have the kitchen and family room flow together. This allows for casual interactions between guests and family members, which is more desirable today than it once was. Ideally, create an area in the kitchen where people can sit and interact. Older, stately homes had smaller kitchens and butler's pantries because servants prepared the meals.

This beach house master bedroom is feminine and formal in a simple way, thanks to a pale color scheme and subtle patters. A beamed, angled ceiling creates a sense of spaciousness, but does not overpower the room.

tion, while the expansive living room was anchored by a giant 36-by-18 foot Persian rug. Theses pieces added another dimension to the home, complementing its complex color schemes and creating proper proportion in its rooms.

Ingrao decorated the dining room with antique wallpaper in a three-dimensional design, which he had found at Christopher Hodsoll, in London. "The room was directed toward a great wall of glass, overlooking the Long Island Sound," the designer remembers. "To balance the Sound's great expanse, I introduced an 18th-century wall covering from China which gave the space warmth and made it seem larger."

The home's elegant light fixtures are both antiques and reproductions, selected to enhance the 18th-century design scheme and temper the scale of the rooms. To create a dramatic focal point in the double-height entry, Ingrao hung a gigantic William IV brass chandelier with nearly 30 arms. Crystal chandeliers and wall sconces also enlivened the living room, dining room and master bedroom. Bell jars and large bronze and glass lanterns decorate the home's less formal spaces.

Accessories provided a finishing touch. Ingrao carefully selected a wide variety of items that included antique porcelain lamps, mahogany urns, oil paintings and antique engravings. Over-scaled tabletop accessories were chosen for large rooms, and both fine and folk art paintings were added to the walls.

## The Summer Home

When he began designing the summer house, which was designed before the permanent residence, Ingrao's ultimate goal was to create a feeling of comfort. "This house was all about the family living at the beach," he says. "To achieve a casual look, we used early American furniture and rugs." Antique light fixtures and excellent reproductions—including lanterns and bell jars and folk art as accessories—enhance the Americana theme.

"The house was in keeping with the 20th-century vernacular of grand American Colonial architecture," Ingrao asserts. "Unlike its 18th-century counterparts, windows, hallways and the outdoor spaces all become an important part of the structure. It's youthful in the way that the barrier between the indoors and outdoors has been reduced, while the kitchen and family room flow together to suit a modern lifestyle."

Scale was also an issue here, given that the clients wanted large, airy rooms filled with natural light. To temper their size, Ingrao installed eye-catching architectural details, including tongue-and-groove and crossbeam ceilings, generous (yet straightforward) moldings, simple recessed panels and oak floors. Furniture was large, upholstered and covered in easy-to-care for cotton. The end result: A house that looks well-appointed, but feels caual.

Regardless of the style Ingrao uses in his designs, he always manages to create new homes that mix the best of yesterday with the best of today. The spaces he creates possess the beauty and refinement of antique historic homes, but are more relaxed.

In other words, they perfectly suit the way we live now.

An antique or reproduction area rug is a novel way to anchor an expansive bathroom while enriching a space filled with new fixtures, fittings and tile.

# FLOORING

1.

2.

3.

*Flooring can add tremendous character to new spaces. While fresh wood can be aged convincingly, it's not hard to find salvaged and distressed wood, which can be especially charming. Two outlets listed below sell reclaimed wood in showrooms across the country, and you can ask local home supply stores and contractors for sources as well. Stone and ceramics can also add a vintage touch to floors: Salvaged stone is sold by a handful of retailers, and there are hundreds of stone and ceramic patterns on the market. Porcelain imitation "stone" looks like the real thing and may be a less expensive option. If you'd rather keep your existing flooring, consider hiring a local painter to create faux barn floors, Aubusson rugs or inlay and parquet patterns. With a talented artisan, any design is possible.*

**ARTISANS: LUCRETIA MORONI, FATTO A MANO** 1, 2, 3

Both an artisan and an interior designer, multitalented Lucretia Moroni decorates her clients' homes with items she makes herself, from custom fabrics and wallpaper to mosaics and frescoes. "The truth is, I'm a decorator who hates to shop," Moroni says from her studio in lower Manhattan. "So I end up customizing everything for my clients. I design rooms that are original and colorful, inspired by European design."

When creating floor patterns, Moroni frequently paints intricate faux wood inlays and faux Persian and Islamic rugs. For a recent job at Manhattan's Russian consulate, she decorated a ballroom floor with an elaborate wooden inlay, incorporating a lily design that echoed the rich, golden-flecked flowers on the room's paneled walls. "The oil paint we used was mixed with a transparent medium that allowed the floor's wooden grain to show through and appear like real inlay," the artist explains.

Trained as a decorative painter at Brussels' prestigious Van der Kelen School, Moroni apprenticed with Milan's venerable architecture and design firm, Renzo Mongiardino, then worked on stage sets for Franco Zeffirelli. In the early 1980s, she moved to New York and began working as a decorative painter and designer on both public and private projects, including the early 1990s renovation of Central Park's Bethesda Fountain Arcade. For that project, Moroni painted 24 large slabs of Botticino marble to resemble colorful stone inlays and bas-reliefs. In 1997, she launched her design firm, Fatto a Mano—Italian for "made by hand." Moroni's fabrics and wallpaper are available through A.M. Collections. For more information on this source, see the section on textiles. To the Trade. **Call 212-686-4848 or visit www.fatto-a-mano.com.**

## COMPANY IN FOCUS: ARTISTIC TILE 4, 5, 6

In the 16 years since Nancy Epstein founded Artistic Tile, the tile industry has undergone a revolution— due in no small part to her innovations. A former stay-at-home mom and part-time Parsons School of Design student, Epstein was working for a cabinetmaker when she came up with the idea of selling tile with kitchen and bath products. When her boss rejected the idea, she started her own company. Her first innovation: Opening a high-end tile store to retail customers, something rarely done at the time. Her second: Building a collection of "rooms" so that customers could see what the product looked like when installed.

Today, Artistic Tile carries over 100 collections made from stone, porcelain, ceramic, glass, metal, cement, leather and cork. Owner Epstein frequently travels the world searching for inspiration and compelling new products. "Many people seem to be longing for roots," she muses. "The materials of the earth are solid, timeless, and help bring a grounded quality to home design. When it comes to tile and stone, true luxury is directly tied to artistry and hand-craftsmanship. There is an intimate quality to items that are crafted by hand."

One of Epstein's recent introductions is leather tile, which develops a lovely, aged patina after installation and can be used in any space so long as it doesn't get wet. Artistic Tile has six U.S. showrooms and is carried in 100+ others across the country; catalogs are also available. For more information on this source, see the section on plumbing. Retail and To the Trade. **Call 800-260-8646 or visit www.artistictile.com.**

4.

5.

6.

## TILE

### PEACOCK PAVERS

Alabama's Peacock Pavers makes concrete tiles that are as attractive and full of character as ancient Italian limestone and travertine. Designers praise this company's product, an inexpensive substitute for natural stone that was created about 15 years ago by former concrete company executive Don Gordon and his wife, Ann. The couple was experimenting with smooth concrete surfaces when they created the character-rich Paver, which has since caught the attention of high-end designers and celebrities such as Sela Ward and Clint Black. The tiles come in eight different sizes, with coordinating trim pieces, and can be custom-colored or ordered in stock hues (buff, champagne, rice white and dolphin gray). Contact the company for samples. Retail. **Call 800-264-2072 or visit www.peacockpavers.com.**

1.

2.

3.

**COUNTRY FLOORS**
Country Floors was founded in the early 1960s by still-life photographer Norman Karlson. At the time, the U.S. market was glutted with four-inch tiles, and lacked the colorful, handcrafted, rustic versions so popular in Europe. Seeing a void, Karlson began selling imported hand-painted and terra-cotta pieces from his small basement-level shop in Manhattan. Today, his company has seven showrooms—each brimming with hundreds of products—and he is credited with transforming the U.S. tile industry. Karlson's current line includes a host of newly manufactured pieces as well as a selection of his original designs. Country Floors' Olde English ceramic tiles draw on medieval motifs and feature a gently pitted, stone-like patina that give them a sense of history, while its Tunisian Baba Chic mosaics combine limestone, terra-cotta and glazed ceramic shards to evoke the rich history of the North African coast. For simple, rusticated stone floors, the company offers porcelain faux "stone" and terra-cotta, which require less maintenance than natural stone. The porcelain imitations are so successful, you won't be able to tell the difference. Retail and To the Trade. **Call 800-311-9995 or visit www.countryfloors.com.**

**PARIS CERAMICS** 1
Despite its name, Paris Ceramics is largely known for its premium-quality antique stone, which lends a sense of age to any space it graces. The company's salvaged stone is generally imported from Europe and the Middle East; its most popular products include centuries-old Jerusalem limestone and antique terra-cotta, though one-of-a-kind reclaimed floors are also in high demand. Paris Ceramics quarries its own stone abroad, and carries hand-painted decorative and glazed tile, as well as marble mosaics and cosmati patterns. There are nine showrooms in the U.S. and one in England. For more information about this source, see the section on architectural salvage. Retail and To the Trade. **Call 888-845-3487 or visit www.parisceramics.com.**

**ANN SACKS** 2, 3
Ann Sacks carries a wide selection of stone and tile flooring, all of which add considerable warmth to a home. One of her newest, and most intriguing, items is black Java limestone, reclaimed from the Southeast Asian island. Originally quarried in mid-1800s Belgium, the stone was used as ballast on merchant ships headed to the Spice Islands. When the ships reached Java, it was unloaded to make room for goods headed back

to Europe. For a century and a half, the stone served as tile in wealthy merchants' homes, where the feet of island inhabitants left it with a rich patina. But Sacks' newest product lines are just as intriguing: Caracol oxblood copper planks that capture the depth and richness of studded wood flooring, with a fresh update; layered and ancient-looking pieces from Italian glass tile manufacturer Bisazza, which boast a modern edge; and Anticosti Mosaics, with a tartan pattern reminiscent of Burberry's classic plaid. Retail. **Call 800-278-8453 or visit www.annsacks.com.**

4.

## WOOD

### PIONEER MILLWORKS 4

Pioneer Millworks sells wood with a past. This Farmington, NY, company offers a wealth of reclaimed flooring, timbers and millwork—and some pretty interesting stories. Its Antique Eastern White and Red Pine Staple were reclaimed from old industrial buildings, while the Heart Pine bears black-rimmed nail holes, indicating its previous life as floorboards and support beams. Jarrah hails from the Australian wool mills, with the look of rainforest-grown mahogany, and Settlers' Plank once belonged to old barns located in the Northeast and along the Ohio River Valley. "When we work with reclaimed timber, we saw it to size and clean it to remove a certain amount of the distressed surface," explains marketing manager Iain Harrison. "The contrast between clean and distressed wood creates more texture, which works well with its other scars and markings." Pioneer Millworks can fashion reclaimed wood to meet its customers' unique needs; its only "fresh-sawed" product is Wide-Plank Eastern White Pine, available in widths up to 20 inches. The lumber is sold through 11 dealers in the U.S. and Canada; a catalog and samples are also available. For more information on this source, turn to the architectural salvage section. To the Trade and Retail. **Call 800- 951-9663 or visit www.pioneermillworks.com.**

5.

6.

### PATINA OLD WORLD FLOORING 5, 6

Patina specializes in the reproduction of vintage European floors. It fashions new hardwoods—white oak, maple and larch—into wide, rustic planks, French parquet patterns and custom medallions. To age the wood, craftsmen hand-scrape each board. Surface distressing comes in three gradations, ranging from small imperfections to surface gouges, hole and dents. A catalog and samples are available. Retail. **Call 800-501-1113 or visit www.patinafloors.com.**

# CHAPTER 9

ANN LECONEY

# BERMUDA COTTAGE

Stepping into interior designer Ann LeConey's enchanting Manhattan townhouse is like taking a jaunt to 19th-century London. The rooms are small and wonderfully busy, bursting with everything English. The walls are dressed in proper British wallpaper and the windows are topped with elaborate silk swags. Framed antique architectural and coat of arms prints cover the walls. The overstuffed English Country furniture is formally arranged. There are several sterling tea services and a staggering collection of Staffordshire figurines on display. The only indications that one hasn't actually stepped back in time are the framed photos of LeConey with an assortment of 21st-century celebrities.

LeConey is known for her ability to combine many periods from many countries into one eclectic interior, but—like her mentor, famed interior designer Mario Buatta—she is something of an Anglophile. So when a longtime client asked LeConey to design a Bermuda cottage home, she knew it would be a breeze—the style was first developed by English colonists in the 17th century.

The client had recently bought a late 20th-century Bermuda cottage style vacation home in Palm Beach, FL, which he wanted gutted and redesigned. "He had been an architecture student for a number of years, so he had very specific ideas about what he wanted in this home," LeConey recalls. "But shortly after he hired me, he realized that we would not be able to achieve his dream in the existing home. It was razed, and we started from scratch."

Despite its larger size, this home retains the charm of the original 17th-century Bermuda cottages due to its white tiled roof, capped chimney and stucco facade.

*"Although scale is generally a problem with today's new high-end homes, this home was specifically designed for a client who didn't want to feel dwarfed in his own house"*

Palm Beach-based architect Jeff Smith was hired, and he and LeConey began a process that would take several years. The result of their collaboration is an 8,000-square-foot home perched just steps from the beach. The exterior is pure Bermuda cottage, with all of the authentic details, including solid rectangular massing, stucco façade, balconies and capped chimneys. While the overall structure is larger than than the original Bermudian homes, very few of its rooms are built on the grand scale the exterior suggests.

"Although scale is generally a problem with today's new high-end homes, this home was specifically designed for a client who didn't want to feel dwarfed in his own house," LeConey explains.

Since she didn't need to design around an oversized space, LeConey was able to focus on antiquing it. She chose five historical styles around which to dress the rooms: Bermuda cottage and Palm Beach styles for the architectural elements and English Country, British colonial and Chinese Chippendale for the decorative aspects. "Combining styles that work harmoniously together is the best way to achieve newly old design," says LeConey. "The last thing you want is for the home to look like a museum."

## Bermuda Cottage Style

The home's interior architectural elements were most influenced by the laid-back Bermuda cottage aesthetic. Original Bermuda cottages were colonial in spirit, with wide-planked wooden floors, paneled or plastered walls, simple moldings and large fireplaces. Limestone was frequently used, as was cedar.

LeConey's choice of materials and architectural elements helped reinforce the Bermuda cottage theme. The home's exposed timber ceilings were made of cedar, and its

**Above:** This living room is capped by a cedar ceiling. Its warm, dark tone makes the ceiling appear less lofty, and conveys the home's Bermuda cottage style.

**Opposite:** A Chinese Chippendale-inspired banister lends an informal air to this two-story space. The same style is on view in the dining room, where it works to unify the home's overall design.

Designers have an arsenal of tricks that make oversized rooms seem cozier. LeConey and Smith built large, arched French doors to minimize towering walls, and added the bull's eye windows near the roofline to help break up the massive space and allow more light to enter the room.

## DESIGNER TIPS

**Bring Colloborators Together From the Start:** When a project requires both an architect and an interior designer, have them work together immediately. It makes the designer's job easier, and will alleviate the need for expensive alterations once the project is completed. LeConey had the architect lower some windows to leave room for window treatments, and persuaded him to use French doors instead of sliding ones. "Architects are great at what they do," she says. "But if they don't know what the interior design is going to be, they can't customize the windows and doors to suit those plans."

**Address Scale:** Today's houses are usually larger than predecessors, so you'll need to address the difference in scale. *Elements of Living's Big Home, Big Challenge: Design Solutions for Larger Spaces* by Kira Wilson Gould is a great resource for fostering intimacy in large spaces.

**Combining Styles:** Avoid imitating just one historic style in your design sheme. Instead, combine several complementary ones to create beautiful, yet fresh settings. If you are not sure which design styles to combine, pick a country and study its history of design. Then choose one style from each century.

**Make Sure Eras Match:** To make your style choices, photocopy a selection of furniture and architectural elements from each era you're considering. Tack up the photocopies and remove the ones that don't work with the group. By eliminating what doesn't work, you will quickly find out what does.

**Bring Things up to Date:** Adapt historic styles to the needs of your contemporary home. For example, if your kitchen and dining room are part of one large space, you may have to make some strategic changes to your basic style guidelines.

**Balance Elements:** When you look through your photocopies, keep an eye out for repeating shapes (squares, circles and curves, etc.). Repetition creates visual harmony, while opposing shapes create positive visual tension. The goal is to have an interesting balance of the two design elements.

**Use Architectural Shells:** When LeConey was planning the Palm Beach home, she started by designing what she calls the "interior architectural shell," which includes all elements of the walls, windows and floors. Start by choosing the wall finishes (paint, plaster, wallpaper or paneling), then focus on window and door shapes and their treatments (shutters, blinds or fabric). Finally, select your flooring material, (wood, tile, stone, carpet or area rugs). Once you've created your architectural shell, select the color scheme, fabrics, furniture and decorative accessories. "Without a strong shell, a space looks incomplete," LeConey explains.

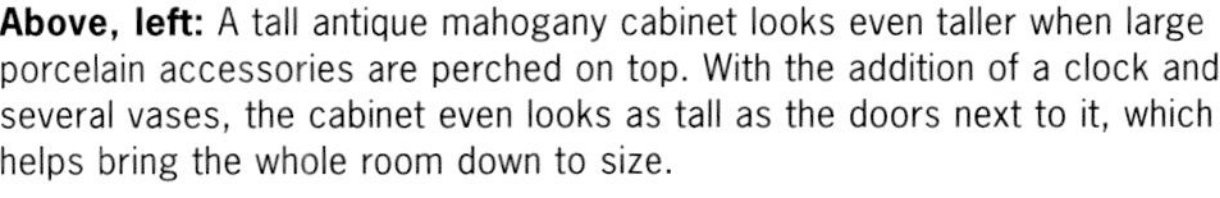

**Above, left:** A tall antique mahogany cabinet looks even taller when large porcelain accessories are perched on top. With the addition of a clock and several vases, the cabinet even looks as tall as the doors next to it, which helps bring the whole room down to size.

**Above, right:** Overstuffed furniture and cushions and equestrian paintings and porcelain give this living room an English look. Most of the room's items were purchased in Enland and shipped over, including an antique side table supported by a hand-cast dolphin—just the thing for a Florida beach house.

pine floors were stained the same color. The library was paneled, the walls were plastered and traditional moldings were added. Limestone tiles covered the floors material in the large, airy entranceway and powder room. "We adapted the Bermudian cottage style to work in this home which, like some new homes, is built on a larger scale than the typical style it mimics," says LeConey. "We had to carefully oversize the elements."

This library's panels are made from pecky cypress, common in Palm Beach homes. Here it gives a warm, informal feeling to what could have been a stuffy, traditional room. Faux leopard-covered armchairs lend personality and contrast nicely with the traditional plaid balloon shades.

## Palm Beach Style

Palm Beach design is known for its tropical flair, cool color schemes and use of materials such as bamboo, rattan and pecky cypress. In this home, its pale hues allowed interiors to reflect natural light, but also faded seamlessly into the rich blues and greens of the surrounding landscape. "The setting was beautiful," LeConey remembers. "It felt like the Caribbean. We wanted the interior colors to complement the view—not compete with it."

Some of the rooms shared wide-open arches, so colors were softly blended between them. "We used either Venetian plaster or glazes on the rooms, and timidly altered their colors and finishes to slightly differentiate them, making the walls more interesting," LeConey says.

Venetian plaster was used in the living room, where the walls were buffed to a high, glass-like sheen. "That effect was wonderful," the designer says. "When the sun came in, the entire room was energized. And at night, when the candles were lit, the walls shimmered."

A cozy, tropical loggia opened out onto the pool. Its hipped ceiling was lined with bamboo, which gave it the look of an upscale beachside hut. Bamboo also covered the moldings that shaped the arched French pool doors. Back inside, the library was paneled with pecky cypress, which set an appropriate, yet informal mood for a place of study.

## Furnishing and Decorative Styles

LeConey spread the home's remaining design styles among its furniture and decorative accessories. English Country was prevalent in most rooms; having originated with British weekend homes, the look had an informal grandeur that seemed perfectly appropriate. Its focus on relaxed elegance and comfort was visible in the home's overstuffed, upholstered pieces, needlepoint rugs, and sterling and Chinese porcelain decorations.

British colonial style could be seen in the home's dark wood and rattan furniture and jungle and tropical prints and fabrics. Known as "campaign" or "knock-down" furniture, its pieces were originally designed to travel with English soldiers who ventured off on campaigns during the expansion of the British Empire. "The home's tropical setting called for British

**Top:** Antique-looking pilasters perfectly frame this dining room, while a tall, coffered ceiling (painted white) gives the space an airy feeling. Most of the furniture and architectural elements were custom-made—often essential to an authentic newly old look. The chandeliers support wax candles and are adorned with fanciful dolphins and seashells, adding a dash of whimsy.

**Bottom:** This loggia opens onto the patio, just steps from the pool and beach. Bamboo decorates the ceiling and frames the moldings over the doors, while the room's midnight blue-and-white color scheme is reflected in the furniture's botanical and porcelain fabric. The room is often used in the evening, so its color scheme was designed to blend into the night sky.

**Top:** The hand-carved, ebony-stained canopy bed evokes British colonial style. But the rest of this room is pure English Country, as demonstrated by its floral fabric, needlepoint rug and overstuffed furniture. A white-washed timber roof lends a dash of informality and adds historic architectural detail.

**Opposite, left:** LeConey used British colonial and bamboo-style furniture for many of the bedrooms. In this one, it nicely complements the jungle theme of the cotton fabric bedspread, window treatments, bamboo window shades and furniture and animal prints. **Opposite, right:** Dark wood and rattan furniture give this room a pure British colonial sensibility.

**Keep It Fresh:** Update certain elements of each style so that your rooms don't look antiquated. For example, if you love the straight lines and reserved feel of Sheraton style chairs, have reproductions made to order. But instead of staining them a dark color, whitewash them and choose a modern fabric such as ultrasuede for the seats' upholstery. The effect will be classic, yet fresh.

**Add Whimsy:** Every home needs fanciful elements to give it a personality—you want guests to be delighted and surprised at opportune moments. Chandeliers are a great way to add fun touches. For example, in an informal dining room, install a chandelier with monkeys holding faux candles. Or, in the kitchen, install one with fruit dripping from it instead of crystal. Pick elements that suit the design theme of the room.

**Buy Antiques:** The most effective way to create a newly old space is to buy antiques or have artisans handcraft furniture that looks antique, based on photographs or detailed drawings. If you have furniture made, be very specific about the design and dimensions you want. It is the only sure way for you to get the piece of furniture you imagined. For the Palm Beach home, LeConey shopped mostly in England, buying antiques and commissioning custom-made furniture that she shipped to the U.S.

**Blend Colors:** Minimize visual transitions between open, connected rooms, using complementary colors, furniture styles and architectural details. If you crave variety, design each bedroom in a different style. Unless you live in a loft, bedrooms rarely have direct transitions from one to the next.

colonial design," LeConey explains. "It is one of the most informal English styles, and its rattan and loose pillows make it well-suited to beach house."

Adding a dash of "required whimsy" to the mix, LeConey based the home's dining room on England's historic Brighton Pavilion. "The Pavilion is so imaginative and playful," the designer says. "It was a folly built for a king. I wanted the dining room to have a similar sense of humor because the client did not want a traditionally formal dining area."

To pull if off, LeConey thought of Thomas Chippendale, the famed 18th-century furniture maker who was inspired by the intricate latticework of Chinese designs for his iconic line of furniture. She filled the dining room with custom-made Chinese Chippendale-inspired pieces, including chairs with latticed backs and a table whose legs bear an applied latticework design. The furniture was whitewashed (to better suit a Florida home) and dark wooden antiques were added for visual contrast. Other fanciful elements included mirrors adorned with tiny bells, chandeliers that held wax candles and a delightful, damask-inspired wall stencil.

"The dining room was meant to amuse," LeConey explains. "There was a tongue-in-cheek aspect to its design, which was refreshingly different from other Palm Beach dining rooms."

Truth be told, the entire house was a refreshing change. Most of its rooms were built on a human scale, and those that were not were made intimate by virtue of its innovative design. LeConey turned to a variety of design styles, but they all mingle seamlessly throughout the home, creating an environment that is (as requested) both comfortable and well-appointed. Although brand-new, the home truly looks like an antique—albeit one that has been impeccably maintained. "I felt like we avoided all of the problems you see in new homes," LeConey says. "The scale worked and the design appeared authentic, but it didn't seem like a historic duplication. It didn't look *new,* which was precisely what we were trying to avoid."

# CARPETS & AREA RUGS

*Fine antique and reproduction rugs add a sense of history to new spaces. Yet modern interpretations of ancient designs are also becoming popular. Many established carpet manufactures are now turning out clean, fresh versions of the historically inspired carpets they have sold for years—and a number of new players are revolutionizing the market as well. The following manufacturers and dealers are among designers' favorites for antique, reproduction and updated traditional rugs. (Keep in mind that antique rug dealers generally offer cleaning and restoration services; designers say the better the dealer, the better its services.)*

1.

**ARTISANS: SARAH GAYLE CARTER** 1, 2, 3

American decorative artist Sarah Gayle Carter produces handcrafted, looped area rugs that take a whimsical approach to ancient design. Her 10-year-old line is both classic and new, with an interesting array of stylized botanical and animal motifs, reproduced in exaggerated forms. The Pedigree rug features exquisite greyhounds, the Black Forest crawls with grizzly bears and Sea Scrolls—inspired by Renaissance stonework—swims with fish and turtles. Madonna Cope, a tapestry of ribbons and roses, was inspired by Italian embroidery. Like all of Carters' rugs, it was made to order. Collections can be custom-cut and -colored to meet a client's needs, but complete custom design is also available. Retail and To the Trade. **Call 804-648-7877 or visit www.sarahgaylecarter.com.**

2.

3.

**COMPANY IN FOCUS: THE RUG COMPANY** 4, 5, 6

In 1997, Christopher Sharp was producing documentaries in the Middle East when he and wife Suzanne came up with an idea for a new kind of carpet business. Their London-based Rug Company has since revolutionized the industry with its unorthodox designs, modern, handmade rugs and wall hangings, and stellar collection of traditional carpets. Many of the contemporary designs offer a fresh take on predictable patterns—generally enlarged, stylized versions of age-old design motifs, presented with fresh colors and textures. In 2000, The Rug Company launched a Designer Collection line, featuring work from leading fashion designers such as Diane von Furstenburg, Paul Smith and Lulu Guinness. The company's more traditional offerings include Aubussons, Ushaks and

Savonneries, but it also sells antique rugs. Products can be seen at The Rug Company's Manhattan showroom; there is also a website and catalog. Retail. **Call 212-274-0444 or visit www.therugcompany.info/newyork/index.**

**ODEGARD**

In the mid-1980s, Stephanie Odegard introduced a line of Tibetan hand-knotted carpets—simplified, abstract versions of traditional carpet designs, generally devoid of borders and restrained in color. Designers consistently praise the craftsmanship of these rugs, which add a desirable richness and worn silkiness to interiors. Although many of Odegard's designs are contemporary, her Abu line works well in traditional interiors, as many of its pieces—including Cloud Oushak, Halloe Metok, Borlu and Velvet Oushak—feel like chenille and look like faded Oriental rugs. But Odegard is as well-respected for her business practices as she is for her stylish products: A former Peace Corps volunteer who once worked at the World Bank and the United Nations, she now focuses on helping developing countries preserve their crafts by marketing them to the U.S. The Odegard collection is on view at 10 U.S. showrooms and at a discount outlet in Long Island City, NY; there is also a company website and catalog. To the Trade. **Call 800-670-8836 or visit www.odegardinc.com.**

**FJ HAKIMIAN** 7, 8

FJ Hakimian has offered decorative carpets and tapestries since the 1970s. The company's vintage rug collection ranges from 18th-century carpets to 1940s Art Deco pieces, with a huge selection that includes Aubussons, Savonneries and Bessarabians, as well as needlepoints from France, India, Turkey, Russia, Africa, Scandinavia and elsewhere. Sizes vary, too—from small area rugs to oversized versions as wide as 40 feet. The company's handmade custom carpets are of heirloom quality, and its artisans can adapt period rug designs to fit any space or color scheme. Customers come toting their own designs or choose from Hakimian's extensive collection of patterns, which dates back to the 17th century. An excellent conservation department also employs about 20 conservators and weavers, many trained in Europe, who can administer first aid to valuable antique rugs. Carpets can be seen on the company's website or (by appointment) at its Manhattan showroom. Retail. **Call 212-371-6900 or visit www.fjhakimian.com.**

4.

5.

6.

7.

8.

**ASMARA** 1, 2, 3
Antique textile and carpet patterns are behind many of Asmara's beautiful rugs, which are famed for their dimension, patina and color. The Asmara Fresco™ technique uses several different colors of ultra-fine thread to create each strand of carpet yarn, producing a complex, subtle shading like that of 16th-century Renaissance fresco. (Asmara's Pavilion and Blue Summer patterns, which contain up to 300 colors apiece, are also made with this technique.) The Savonile™ weave, by contrast, combines variegated flat and pile threads for a surface that resembles antique Italian cut velvet. All carpets are hand-knotted and tufted by artisans in China, and many take up to nine months to produce. Products are available on the company website, and through 100+ U.S. dealers. Retail and To the Trade. **Call 800-451-7240 or visit www.asmarainc.com.**

**STARK CARPETS** 4, 5
For nearly 70 years, Stark Carpet has set the standard for fine traditional carpeting. The company was founded in 1935 by Arthur and Nadia Stark, who noticed a dearth of antique European and reproduction rugs in the U.S. market. Their sons, John and Steven, now carry on the family business, with thousands of broadlooms and other carpets that range from antiques and period reproductions to historically inspired and custom-designed pieces. Stark's wool Germaine broadloom was modeled after a floral tapestry that graced a Scottish castle, while its plaid-and-checked Shetland Scotch Ingrain broadloom is reminiscent of a flat-weave style popular during the Victorian era. The equally innovative Veronica collection blends 18th-century Aubusson and Savonnerie floral patterns and manufacturing techniques. The company's distressed leather rugs are based on antique flooring patterns. There are 31 U.S. showrooms, as well as a company website and catalog. To the Trade. **Call 212-752-9000 or visit www.starkcarpet.com.**

**ABRAHAM MOHEBAN & SON, INC.**
Founded in 1961 by Persian-born Abraham Moheban, this family-run company is considered one of Manhattan's best sources for fine antique Oriental and European rugs. Moheban was just a teenager when he started working in the industry, and designers credit him as one of the pioneers of the U.S. rug trade. His showroom offers Savonnerie, Aubusson, Axminster, Sultanabad, Kerman and Kashan carpets in standard, non-standard and oversized versions; he also cleans, restores, repairs and appraises antique carpets. Retail. **Call 212-758-3900 or visit www.moheban.com.**

**RENAISSANCE CARPET & TAPESTRIES**
New York–based Renaissance is an excellent source for high-end Aubusson and Savonnerie-style carpets and tapestries. Intricate, colorful, and multidimensional, its collection reproduces 17th-century pieces and those found in period documents. Their authenticity owes no small debt to production manager and chief artist Philippe Hecquet, the former owner of a prestigious manufacturing facility in Aubusson, France (established by his family in 1762). A sample of the company's carpets can be seen on its website; there are showrooms across the U.S. To the Trade. **Call 800-325-7847 or visit www.renaissancecarpet.com.**

**SCHUMACHER** 6, 7
Founded over a century ago, Schumacher started out as an importer of high-end, decorative fabrics from Europe. It introduced a carpet line in the 1930s, and now boasts a wealth of original, antiques-inspired patterns and designs based on historical documents. The company is perhaps best known for its Wilton carpet, a circa-18th-century design with a loop weave and coordinating fields and borders. New Wilton collections include Lokins Floral, which features botanical designs (e.g. scattered vines) inspired by archival documents, Rainbow Trellis, based on historical patterns and displaying either a large-scale trellis or scattered bouquets, and Rutherford, which comes in damask or falling leaf patterns, set against a white or red background. Schumacher's four staff artists are

1. 2. 3.

constantly developing new carpet lines, and work with designers to customize them; the company's products can be seen in showrooms across the U.S. For more information on this source, see the section on textiles. To the Trade. **Call 212-415-3900 or visit www.fschumacher.com.**

4.

**KARASTAN**

Karastan has been producing affordable, attractive reproduction rugs for over 70 years. The company's machine-made carpets come in a wide variety of styles, including modern reinterpretations of ancient motifs and straightforward period recreations. Notable collections include English Manor, Antique Legends and Persian Renaissance. English Manor's William Morris is a striking standout: Paying homage to England's circa-1880s Arts and Crafts movement, it bears an intricate flora-and-foliage pattern reminiscent of Morris' own rich, layered style (itself inspired by 17th-century European textiles and ancient Persian design). The Antique Legends Collections' Agra is also a stunner, with rich-looking leaves and palmettes inspired by Indian carpet design. And Ziegler features vine patterns surrounded by wide borders, based on a popular 19th-century Persian rug style. Its soothing color palette and tranquil design compliment both traditional and contemporary rooms. Karastan rugs are sold by 100+ U.S. retailers; carpets can be seen on the company's website and in its catalog. Retail. **Call 800-234-1120 or visit www.karastan.com.**

5.

6.

7.

Gambrel's youthful version of a traditional Jeffersonian farmhouse retains the style's historical character while stripping it of extraneous decorative details.

# CHAPTER 10

STEVEN GAMBREL

# OLD GLORY

Steven Gambrel's clients tend to be self-made young, urban professionals like him, which is why there is often a generous dollop of cool to his designs. But the University of Virginia-trained architect isn't just about urban chic: His work, so perfect for the young, can also be right for the young-at-heart. In fact, Gambrel was recently hired to build a suburban home for new retirees, working in a style he'd never done before.

Of course, the clients happened to be Gambrel's parents. And the inspiration behind the home's design, a classic Jeffersonian farmhouse, was a seemingly natural fit for the Virginia native. But even with this inside edge over other designers, he was the perfect choice to create the home. Having spent over a decade working as an interior designer, and with an architectural background, Gambrel knew how to both build and decorate a space that would meet his parents needs.

Gambrel began the design by taking long rides through his home state's countryside, giving himself a refresher course in local architecture. He also consulted books on Palladian and Jeffersonian style architec-

The sparing use of exotic woods, fine marble and classic hardware lent a sense of grandeur to many Colonial American homes.

*"The whole concept was not to **salvage** old pieces or **distress** materials, but instead to use **honest,** timeless **natural** materials including wood, honed marble and slate which would **age gracefully** over time and become old by their inherent **character.**"*

This front entranceway creates a dramatic first impression with a marble checkered floor, mahogany doors and light walls.

ture. Thomas Jefferson designed some of Virginia's best known architectural treasures, including its state university. His famous home, Monticello, was based on theories of proportion and design espoused by 16th-century Renaissance architect Andrea Palladio. Widely copied throughout Virginia, Monticello is a masterpiece of Palladian stateliness, featuring impressive exteriors, economic use of materials and a harmony between the indoor and outdoor realms. It was these aspects that Gambrel sought to incorporate in his parents' new home.

"When I was touring Virginia, I realized that a lot of Jeffersonian farmhouses looked modern, because they were sparse and undecorated," he remembers. "They had classic proportions and tall ceilings, and were constructed from humble materials. Yet they were dressed up with generous moldings and fenestrations."

## Small, but Grand

Gambrel's goal was to build his parents a "grand small" house. "Unlike builders' homes, which can have too much square footage, grand small homes are successful because they have generous proportions, but few rooms," the designer explains. "For this project we wanted to use the Palladian proportions of a Virginia farmhouse, but slightly update them and clean them up. We also wanted to give the house a youthful quality."

The end result was a 2,300-square-foot house with a large, two-story central hall and two symmetrical wings. Classic in form, the house was suited to modern life, with the ground floor devoted to the couple's living quarters and the second floor set aside for guests. The two floors used different heating and cooling systems, so the upstairs could be closed off when no one was visiting.

"Living on the first floor is a Colonial American idea," says Gambrel. "People used to basically live in one large room. Creating a living space on the ground floor is ideal for a couple who plan to grow old in a home." (In other words, there are fewer stairs to climb.)

Unlike other designers, Gambrel didn't use reclaimed materials or age new ones to create this home's authentically antique interior. "The whole concept was not to salvage old pieces or distress materials but instead to use honest, timeless, natural ones including wood, honed marble and slate, which would age gracefully over time and become old by their inherent character," he explains.

Additionally, Gambrel used these natural materials when constructing the home, rather than applying them merely as decoration. "Many new spaces fail to look authentically antique because the builders simply tack on architectural elements rather than building them into the structures," Gambrel says. "Materials such as wide wooden planks with natural grooves and knots have spirit. Their spirit becomes part of the room."

**Top:** To temper this living room's 11-foot ceilings, Gambrel installed amply proportioned windows and filled one wall with artwork, hung in an old world way with small chains from a bronze rod.

**Bottom:** The living room is designed in a clean, classic way. To add a youthful quality, Gambrel used solid fabrics instead of richly textured or patterned ones. Gus, another of the family's Labradors, snoozes in front.

DESIGNER TIPS

**Think Grandly Small:** When building your home, consider the Jeffersonian concept of "grand small." Grand small homes have less square footage and fewer rooms than the norm, but their rooms are generously sized, with tall ceilings and amply proportioned moldings.

**Display Art Salon-Style:** When hanging art, consider doing so in a salon style: Hang multiple paintings from a bronze rod with chains. They can fill an entire wall and lends a room a highly-styled and old world look.

**Create Heating/Cooling Zones:** To conserve energy and save money, section off areas of the home that aren't used often, and keep separate heating and cooling systems. It sounds like a new idea, but early Americans commonly lived in one area of the home.

**Use Fine Materials Structurally:** Honest, timeless materials such as wooden planks, slate tile and marble will age gracefully overtime. Build rooms from these materials rather than using them as surface decoration. When built into the structures (i.e., using planks to construct walls), quality materials make a space look authentically antique.

**...And Use Them Strategically:** If used sparingly in important areas of the home, metalwork and fine woods such as mahogany give a space a sense of rural grandeur without being too costly. The first thing any visitor sees is the entry hall. Make it a knockout.

## Strategically Using Fine Materials

According to Gambrel, rural Jeffersonian homes are typically noted for their sparing use of fine wood species and metal work in critical spaces. The designer chose the same approach for his parent's house. "We made the entry hall special, to give a strong first impression," he says. "The floors were marble, the moldings generous and the dark mahogany doors eight feet tall. Traditional knuckle hinges were added as hardware."

The two-story front hall featured contrasting, honed, dull marble squares, which were popular in Colonial America. A bell jar light fixture illuminated a traditional, understated stairwell. Large, mahongany doors, topped with a classic pediment, led into the first-floor rooms, where walls were decorated with intriguing art, including French botanical prints and a portrait Gambrel painted of the family's deceased black Labrador, Emma, playfully wearing pearls.

"It was a strong entry, designed in a classic Jeffersonian way," Gambrel acknowledges. "It was detailed, but in a clean, elegant way.

In the living room, Gambrel hung his parent's artwork, salon-style, on a bronze rod and chain. The custom-made fireplace surround was inspired by an antique English mantel while the furniture is a combination of antiques and pieces Gambrel's designed himself. "I wanted the living room to look fresh and current, so the furniture I designed had clean lines and straightforward colors, which contrasted with my parents' collection of dark antiques," he says. "The room looked fashionable, but had historic bones."

This informal breakfast room, located next to the kitchen is rustic and airy—not unlike an early American porch.

Even though it has the latest in appliances, the kitchen is simply designed to evoke a country feeling. A selection of vintage botanical prints and the slate-tiled floor give the room an early American appeal.

## Casual Elegance

Gambrel chose slate flooring for the kitchen, in part because it was easy to clean—an important factor considering that the family's current labrador retriever, Isaac, likes to go for romps in the woods. Even so, slate still adds a historic touch, calling to mind the "great old scullery kitchens of working country houses," says Gambrel

"Bluestone floors are casual—perfect for wet dogs and active families," he continues. "And they age beautifully."

The breakfast room, located just off the kitchen, featured the same slate flooring and look. Its walls were adorned with tongue-and-groove jointed pine boards, which charmingly show their seams. An antique, wrought-iron chandelier sat above a country-style table, where classic Windsor chairs were grouped in mismatched colors. The windows were left bare, accentuating the flow between the indoors and outdoors.

"What I like about the Windsor chairs was that they no longer matched," Gambrel recalls. "A new coat of paint would

**Above, left:** The Hamptons beach house relies on an eclectic selection of furniture and a citrus color scheme to evoke a mid-20th-century look.

**Above, right:** A new home spirit is achieved in this beachouse through a lively color scheme—demonstrated in the hues of the armchair's textile—and its eclectic arrangement of furniture and accessories.

have made them new and color-coordinated, but chairs like this show the evolution of furniture over time."

## Beach Delight

For another project, Gambrel turned a friend's generic builder's home into a character-rich Hamptons beach house. "I was surprised he bought this house, but understood that he liked that everything was new and working," the designer says. "On weekends, he didn't want to contend with the maintenance of the home—he wanted to enjoy it."

The client had two design parameters: He didn't want the house torn down, though he told Gambrel that he could tear it apart. And he didn't want his beach house to resemble a city apartment.

To erase the builder's imprint, Gambrel set about adding architectural elements—gables, working plank-board exterior shutters and a pergola with a fireplace. On the interior, he closed up the open floor plan to create a traditional one, with clear divisions between the rooms. Then, to liven up its plain sheetrock walls, he added moldings and tongue-and-groove

The beach house's formal dining room is simply designed. To remove the builder's imprint, Gambrel installed moldings, wainscoting, strong color and elegantly styled furniture. Treasures from the sea are playfully mounted on the walls.

panels. Finally, the library's walls were covered with wooden planks, making the room seem almost porch-like.

Gambrel decided on a citrus color scheme, preferring it to the typical blue and white that permeates many seaside cottages. He chose a bright and funky palette—tangerine orange, sunburst yellow and lime green—inspired by the wild colors of vintage Pucci dresses. Fashionably striped carpeting was paired with richly patterned textiles in diamond, round and square shapes.

"The idea behind the color scheme and furnishings was the sense that this home might have been owned by a widely traveled, eccentric great aunt, who used it for entertaining in the 1960s, then left it to my client," Gambrel explains. "The house was meant to look as if it hadn't been touched in 40 years."

The furniture is eclectic, a combination of antiques and pieces from the last century. "Beyond the floor plan, I didn't design the house in a 19th-century way," Gambrel says. "I simply wanted it to be fashionable, with a retro appeal. I was thinking of the 1971 film the *Summer of '42* when I designed it." (The film takes a romantic look back at island life on a World War II-era New England island—precisely the sensibility Gambrel wanted for the beach house.)

Artwork added greatly to the home's distinct personality. Gambrel hung framed, antique topographical maps in the library, and mounted a collection of coral and seashells on the walls of the dining room. The collection works nicely with the room's iron chandelier, which also resembled coral tentacles. In a guest bedroom, the designer mounted a fleet of model sailboats, adding a nautical, old world air.

Both houses balanced traditional architecture with fashionable decoration, creating a look that's classic and cool—just like their designer.

The subdued color palette of this beach house sunroom is meant to evoke life on the Riviera, circa 1940. The natural materials of the wooden floor lamp, bamboo chairs and sea grass rug are elegantly juxtaposed with the scalloped valence and tailored sofa.

DESIGNER TIPS

**Blend Furniture:** To keep a room full of antiques from looking too period, mate them with clean, lined, upholstered furniture, covered in plain textiles.

**Make Creative Artwork Choices:** Artwork such as framed antique topographic maps—especially those featuring the area around your home—are appropriate for a beach house. It's a simple way to enrich the interior decoration with a little history. Collectible items, placed on wall brackets, add a note of whimsy to plain sheetrock walls.

**Get Rustic:** If you want to create rooms that look similar to those in early American farmhouses, choose rustic furniture in simple forms.

**Install Shutters:** Antique-looking shutters can transform the façade of a generic-looking builder's home.

**Traditional Floor Plans:** Most people want open floor plans today, but if you want to evoke traditional architecture, divide the open room into distinct spaces. Open plan homes have really only come into vogue in the last few decades.

This guestroom is filled with vintage furniture and nautically inspired textiles. Model ships floating on the walls encourage dreams of ancient mariners.

# HARDWARE

*Good hardware can really add another dimension to a room. Not only does it help establish a home's historic look, but it can turn even the plainest rooms into period settings. Here, we'll look at hardware for furnishings and architecture; see also the sections on windows and plumbings for additional types of hardware. Since it can be expensive, designers suggest that those on a budget save top-shelf pieces for important "public" places—the kitchen, entryway, or entire first floor—and use less-costly items elsewhere. The good news: There are many manufacturers of reproduction and period-inspired hardware, which is often updated in style, material or finish for a novel take on an antique look.*

1.

**ARTISANS: CARL MARTINEZ** 1, 2

Carl Martinez makes inventive decorative hardware, inspired by childhood memories of the metalsmiths who populated bazaars in Iran, where he grew up. Martinez came to America during the Iranian revolution of the late 1970s, earning an architecture degree at the University of New Mexico and making furniture in Miami. He was soon drawn to New York: "When I arrived in Manhattan, I gravitated towards metalwork, because I was so inspired by the city's steel buildings," the designer remembers. Martinez apprenticed with a jewelry-maker and taught himself welding, and in 1992, opened his own Chinatown studio, where he has been handcrafting hardware ever since. His pieces include 24-karat gold-plated doorknobs, zebrawood drawer handles, enamel and metal cabinet pulls, and colorful glass doorknobs, modeled after ancient Venetian glassware and chandeliers. He also fashions window and plumbing hardware, lighting and accessories. Designer Robert Couturier compares his work to sculpture. "I specialize in one-of-a-kind art objects," Martinez explains. "The designs are updated, streamlined and simple—palatable for modern-day customers." Retail. **Call 212-941-8142 or visit www.carlmartinezhardware.com.**

2.

3.

**COMPANY IN FOCUS: P.E. GUERIN** 3, 4

P.E. Guerin pioneered the use of artistic metalwork in the U.S. The family-run company has been manufacturing high-end hardware since the mid-19th century, and is now operated by Andrew F. Ward, its founder's great-grandnephew. The firm remains at the top of designers' hardware lists, noted for its wide range of American and European pieces, including ornate, Louis XV-style drawer pulls, restrained, Georgian-inspired doorknobs, and contemporary-looking plexiglass and metal levers. Custom work makes up the bulk of Guerin's business; stock items are largely made of brass and steel, while both stock and custom finishes are available. All products are handmade and hand-finished using early 20th-century methods. A Manhattan showroom has 25,000+ items in stock (available for viewing by appointment); there are four additional U.S. showrooms and one in Puerto Rico. Products can also be seen on the company's website. For more information on this source, see the section on plumbing. To the Trade. **Call 212-243-5270 or visit www.peguerin.com.**

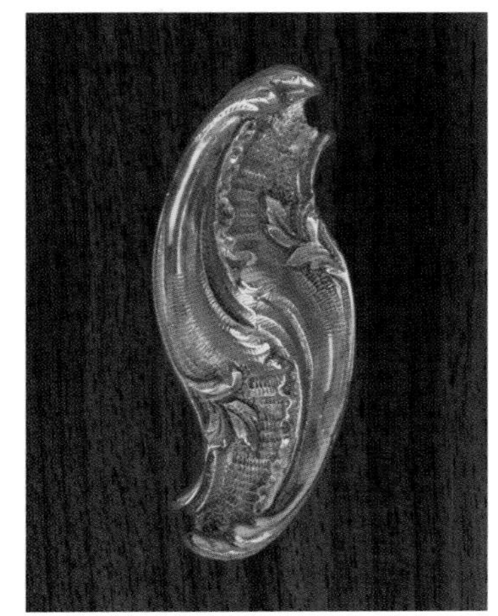

4.

**COMPANY IN FOCUS: RESTORATION HARDWARE** 5, 6

In 1979, Restoration Hardware founder Stephen Gordon was fixing up a Queen Anne Victorian home, and finding it hard to locate authentic period hardware. Sensing a void in the market, Gordon then opened a reproduction store in Eureka, CA, which has since grown into 100+ U.S. stores and a thriving online and mail-order business. His products are fashionable, well-made and accessibly priced, which makes them popular with both interior designers and retail customers. Based on period styles, but lacking excessive decoration, they appeal to modern tastes: Top products include vintage-looking "bin" pulls, Victorian-style amber glass and satin brass hooks (with matching drawer pulls), and Arts and Crafts zinc ring pulls in an antique finish. Retail. **Call 800-762-1005 or visit www.restorationhardware.com.**

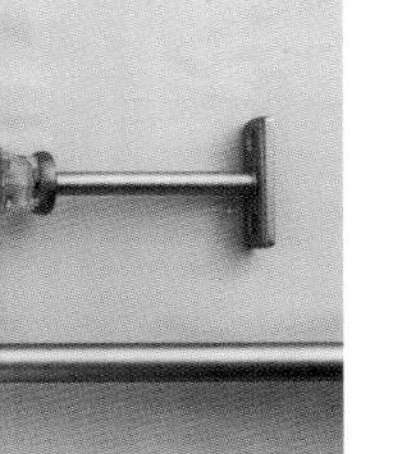

5.

**WHITECHAPEL**

Founded over 15 years ago by English cabinetmaker Bob Dunstan, Whitechapel currently offers 4,200+ high-quality reproductions of period hardware, with items ranging from bed fittings to entry sets and stays. It offers the basics (brass claw casters and harpsichord hinges) as well as more unusual items (vintage brass padlocks, ornate Swiss-style iron hinges, desk mail slots). A catalog is available. Retail. **Call 307-739-9478 or visit www.whitechapel-ltd.com.**

6.

**NANZ** 1, 2

Nanz was founded in the late 1980s by two college friends, Carl Sorenson and Steven Nanz. "At the time, we were refinishing and repairing early 20th-century hardware from prewar Manhattan apartment buildings," Sorenson recalls. "There were never enough pieces, so we started to reproduce them. The patina, heft and craftsmanship of the early hardware is what we try to capture in the items we produce today." The Brooklyn, NY, Nanz factory makes customized, high-end hardware for discerning clients, to whom they offer a choice of materials, styles, sizes and finishes. An extensive online catalog features a wide variety of hinges, knobs, levers, locks, window hardware and cabinet plates. Among their vintage, modern and historically inspired pieces are a spherical, seeded glass doorknob, based on a mid-19th-century design, a classic French escutcheon doorplate with diamond pattern, and a Gothic-inspired lever based on 19th-century neo-Gothic examples. The company's showroom is located in downtown Manhattan. To the Trade. **Call 212-367-7000 or visit www.nanz.com.**

**CROWN CITY HARDWARE**

Located in Pasadena, CA, Crown City Hardware offers 4,000+ top-quality "restoration" pieces. The company sells restored antique hardware and also offers notable hardware collections, including hand-hammered Arts and Crafts and handmade Victorian Windsor pieces, and Depression-era crystal and glass (for cabinets and doors). Finishes include polished nickel, oil-rubbed bronze, highlighted brass and antique copper. A catalog is available. Retail. **Call 800-950-1047 or visit www.restoration.com.**

**THE OLD HOUSE STORE**

Oxfordshire, England's Old House Store is a treasure trove for the renovation-minded, featuring decorative hardware in both traditional and primitive styles. The company manufactures solid brass and iron locks, knobs, hinges and hooks, and even handcrafts traditional rosehead iron nails. Its iron hardware is hand-forged by its own blacksmiths and wax-finished for interior uses. Old House also carries about 200 renovation building product lines, from lime plaster to oak framing pegs. Many products can be seen on the company website and in its catalog; the store can customize orders and will ship anywhere in the world. Retail. **Call +44 (0)11-8969-7711 or visit www.oldhousestore.co.uk.**

**HOUSE OF ANTIQUE HARDWARE**

The House of Antique Hardware boasts 1,400+ pieces of reproduction period hardware, ranging from Victorian-style floor grates to Colonial-style carpet runner rods and push-button light switches with faux mother-of-pearl inlay. The Portland, OR-based company also sells antique hardware and has an extensive collection of nostalgic door sets, dating back in style to the early 1800s. All stock products are available on its website. Retail. **Call 888-223-2545 or visit www.houseofantiquehardware.com.**

**ELLIOTT'S HARDWARE**

Elliott's offers over a thousand pieces of reproduction antique and vintage hardware. Some of the Dallas, TX, company's intriguing items include its tin ceiling tiles, window rope pulleys, Chippendale-inspired keyhole furniture plates and Colonial-styled cabinet hardware. Look under the "Hardware Plus" icon on Elliott's website to search and view products. A catalog is also available. Retail. **Call 214-634-9900 or visit www.elliottshardware.com.**

**REJUVENATION** 3

Like several others on this list, Jim Kelly founded his company after he discovered how difficult it was to locate historic hardware and details. Rejuvenation was born in the 1970s, shortly after Kelly bought and attempted to rehabilitate a condemned

1.

2.

storefront in Portland, OR. He began by selling architectural salvage there, but soon recognized that supply didn't keep up with demand. As a result, Rejuvenation now sells reproductions of American hardware, lighting and plumbing from the 1880s to the 1960s. The business has been a great success: Some of its products adorn the country's greatest landmarks, including New York's Grand Central Station and California's Hearst Castle. Among its finishes are lacquer-free brass and unfinished oil-rubbed bronze (both of which gracefully age to give the hardware an authentic antique patina) and brushed nickel (which resembles stainless steel). Rejuvenation has two large retail stores in Portland and Seattle. For more information on this source, see the chapter on plumbing. Retail. **Call 888-401-1900 or visit www.rejuvenation.com.**

3.

**VAN DYKE'S RESTORERS** 4

For the last 20 years, Van Dyke's Restorers has been selling antique and vintage-inspired home restoration supplies, including over 10,000 pieces of hardware for both architecture and furniture. Products range from Art Nouveau-style brass shelf brackets and copper-finished Victorian hinges to porcelain and glass doorknobs and iron furniture pulls. The company also has curious, hard-to-find items, including classic wall-mounted bottle openers and storage racks from railroad cars. Van Dyke carries Keeler and Armac hardware brands; its own Legacy hardware line is available in 11 finishes and unlacquered brass. A catalog is available. Retail. **Call 800-558-1234 or visit www.vandykes.com.**

4.

**JOSEPH BIUNNO** 5

Famed for its excellent furniture refinishing and restoration, Manhattan's Joseph Biunno also makes window treatment hardware and handcrafts replacement furniture hardware (including keys and locks) to expertly match the originals. For more information about this source, see the sections on window treatments and restored & hand-painted furniture. Retail and To the Trade. **Call 212-629-5630 or visit www.antiquefurnitureusa.com.**

5.

ACCESSORIES

# RESOURCES

1.

2.

3.

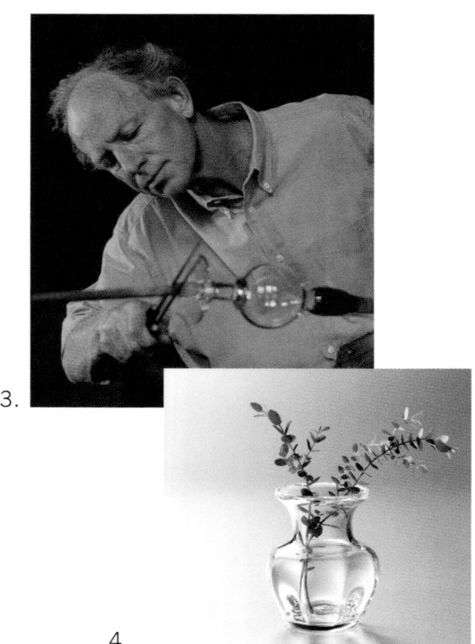

4.

**DESIGNER TIPS: ACCESSORIZING NEW SPACES BY CARL D'AQUINO** 1

When it comes to accessories, my firm always seeks to blend the neoclassic and modern. We love juxtaposing the old and new: Older pieces add elegance to a room, but they also provide a historical context for the later objects—a sense of where they came from.

Scale is very important when accessorizing. In smaller spaces, we often work with oversized antiques, which add a tremendous amount of drama and attract the eye. They throw off the perception of scale in a positive way.

Installing oversized pieces in large spaces has the reverse effect. Placing a large antique stone bust in a big window niche will make the window appear smaller. It's all about proportion. If you are designing for a room with high ceilings, you want accessories to help disguise the scale of the room. Choose larger, taller candlesticks and vessels, and then mate them with some smaller objects.

My favorite collections are the ones that don't look forced. It's best when the clients have added to them little by little over the years. Such collections look natural and are great conversation pieces, because there really is a story behind them. For clients new to collecting or decorating a second home, we encourage them to identify their hobbies and passions—and then we go shopping. Where relevant, we try to gather elements that have an aged appearance to them, which brings an instant vintage look to the collection.

We also want different shapes and sizes, which add texture and create tension. Clients should also amass collections from a variety of countries and time periods, and keep adding to them, so that they mature and grow. And, when displaying, bring uniform accessories together: One of our clients collected blue-and-white porcelain pieces, including a number of small vases, and we placed all of the vessels in a row on a large fireplace mantel. Since the mantel was the focal point in the room, it immediately directed attention to the porcelain.

We also love to display family portraits, and very often create a gallery from them. It's exciting to have family history on display. We generally use bold colors for the collection, such as a red lacquer frame with a deep blue mat. The background colors unify the pictures regardless of whether they are large or small, in color, sepia or black and white. We like to mount them somewhere intimate and out of the way, but we still want guests to see them. Hallways are good, or just outside of powder rooms, or on a stair landing. We give our clients a hanging plan so that they can continue to add to the collection. Another idea is to create a family gallery with free-standing frames placed in built-ins or cabinets. Again, I like to use frames with the same material—all silver, dark wood or enamel—but in different styles and shapes.

**DESIGNER TIPS: SUCCESSFUL TABLETOP DESIGN BY GLENN GISSLER** 2

I approach tabletop design in the same way that I might approach architecture or urban planning: I see it as a universe in and of itself. There has to be a variation of scale and texture for tabletop design to be successful. Proper scale is created when a variety of heights play off of each other. Texture comes from a combination of materials—wood, stone, ceramic, metal, shell or glass. Additional visual interest is created when opposites are mated, such as rough versus smooth, shiny versus matte, round versus square, antique versus modern, and so forth.

When you accessorize a tabletop, you have to take into account the entire scale of the room. If everything in a room is large and oversized, you must include a few larger pieces with your smaller accessories. Placing large, medium and small items together on the table breaks the room's scale down. You must also take into account the furniture you are using as a base for the tabletop design: Be conscious of their material and style, and allow those elements to guide your choice of accessories.

I personally like to organize my tabletops asymmetrically. I find that symmetrical arrangements give immediate satisfaction to the viewer—because they are balanced—but that the feeling quickly disappears and the design becomes dull. Strong symmetry is the deadliest, because it is too static. I also think that it is important to give objects room to breathe. I'm not a fan of busy tabletops. For me, there is nothing worse than a tabletop so jumbled with framed pictures that you can't even see the photos.

Three tabletops I recently created for beach houses demonstrate a few different approaches to designing with accessories:

On a 19th-century Anglo-Indian table in a formal foyer, I placed a collection of 19th-century Mercury glass in a variety of shapes and forms, organized in an asymmetrical way. There was a tall, thin lamp, several vases, a traditional Mercury glass ball and a few very petite items. I hung a framed line drawing just above them to add another form—in this case, a rectangle bordering a rounded, free-flowing design. The metallic frame linked the art with the items on the table, so it became part of the design. Underneath the table, I placed a large rustic clamming basket, in texture the exact opposite of the mirrored Mercury glass. This added a relaxed element to the space. Although all of the table's accessories were metallic, they were offset by the basket, and the whole thing worked well because of the interplay of scale and shape.

On a rustic Anglo-Indian cabinet in an informal living room, I placed a lamp that I had fashioned from an antique wooden metal casting mold next to a short, thin, square silver cup, which served as a vase. In front of the two forms was a low, flat ceramic bowl—1970s hippie art. A simply matted and framed 18th-century engraving was casually left leaning against the wall, and two stacked books completed the scene. Again, the tabletop was successful because of the variety of materials, and the balance of scale and form.

The tabletop pictured here (2) is in a bedroom, so I wanted the majority of the forms to be soft, round and organic. The table was a 19th-century Art Nouveau bentwood with an elegant, sculptural presence. Atop it, I placed a rounded lamp made from a converted vase, a framed shell print supported by a stand, and a rounded, carved stone vessel. The lamp was tall, the print was medium-sized and the vessel was short—an asymmetrical combination. To counterbalance the curves, I chose a rectangular frame and added a small hardcover book. The mixture of materials, forms and scales made the tabletop design interesting.

**ARTISANS: SIMON PEARCE** 3, 4

Few people know that Simon Pearce is a man, as well as a trademark. Before he started the company bearing his name, Pearce studied glass design at the Royal College of Art in London and apprenticed in several European glass houses. (He had grown up learning how to throw clay on a wheel, as his father was a potter by trade.) About 30 years ago, Pearce started his own glassblowing company in Ireland, and a decade later, moved the firm to the U.S. The rest is history. Visitors flock to Pearce's Vermont flagship, located in a restored, historic wool mill, to watch products being made. Glassblowers must work at the company for five to 10 years before being promoted to master level. (The lengthy apprenticeships demonstrate how difficult it is to perfect the craft, explaining why there are always discounted "seconds" for sale at Simon Pearce retail outlets.) "Perfect clarity is the most difficult element to

1.

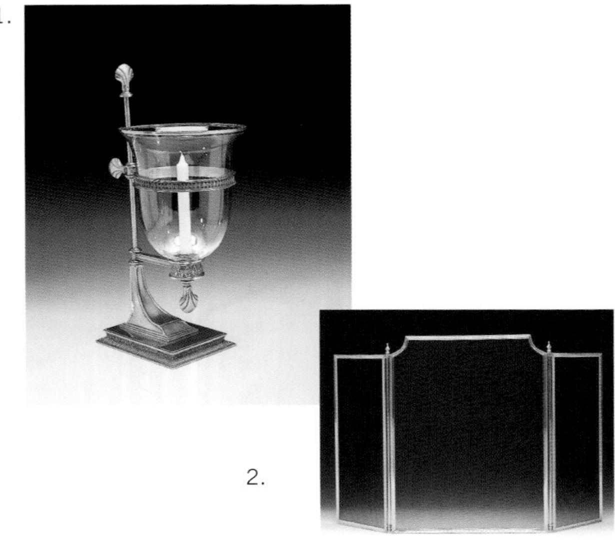

2.

3.

4.

5.

6.

achieve," Pearce offers. "If it's clear, it has to be perfect. One can hide a multiple of sins with colored glass." Designers say Pearce's products are popular because of their familiar, stripped-down forms and simplistic materials, which suit almost any room. Their high quality and affordability has earned them the nickname "Steuben for the Everyman." Products are available at 12 Simon Pearce retail stores, other outlets and on the company website. Retail. **Call 877-452-7763 or visit www.simonpearce.com.**

*After the designers in this book have grown weary of searching antiques stores for accessories, or given up rummaging through their client's closets (looking for long-forgotten or inherited collections), they venture out to these sources, hoping to find the perfect finishing touch:*

**DECORATIVE CRAFTS** 1, 2

For over 75 years, family-run Decorative Crafts has been importing historically inspired, handcrafted goods from Italy. Its accessories are largely made from brass, silver, bronze and tole, and range from hurricane lamps with antiqued brass bases to lacquered brass fireplace screens and tole jars with hand-painted floral designs. The Greenwich, CT, company also sells a wide variety of hand-carved wooden items and hand-painted mirrors influenced by the Empire, Neoclassical, and Louis XIV periods (Venetian hand-etched versions are also available). Decorative Crafts has six showrooms in major U.S. cities; free catalogs can be ordered through its website. For more on this source, see the section on restored & hand-painted furniture. To the Trade or retail through Izolli. (See trade tips section for Izolli contact information.) **Call 800-431-4455 or visit www.decorativecrafts.com.**

**SCULLY & SCULLY** 3, 4

In the 70 years since Scully & Scully opened its doors, it has set the standard for traditional, upscale home décor. Known as New York's "smart" (i.e., fashionable) gift shop, it offers everything from porcelain animal figurines to sterling silver vessels and fabric-upholstered frames. Scully & Scully boasts something for every personality, from hand-sculpted and hand-painted blooming porcelain lilies to playful Viennese bronzes of frogs and dachshunds. The company also sells furniture and tabletop items, and is a great place to pick up tips on accessorizing with taste. A catalog is available. Retail. **Call 800-223-3717 or visit www.scullyandscully.com.**

**ALAN MOSS**
Alan Moss sells high-quality 20th-century American and European decorative accessories, lighting, furniture and architectural salvage. Known for its Italian art glass and sculpture, Moss carries an eclectic selection of products that includes Gilbert Poillerat-designed bronze-and-iron andirons and a Jean Despres-designed tea service. In business for 30 years, it is also an excellent source for Art Deco and Art Moderne furniture, especially mirrored pieces. Retail. **Call 212-473-1310 or visit www.alanmossny.com.**

**WILLIAM-WAYNE & CO.**
Under the name William-Wayne & Co., William Meyer and Wayne Adler run two very tasteful shops in Manhattan. They opened the stores to fill a distinct niche in the design world: "Our clients' homes are typically filled with beautiful antiques and tabletop goods," says Meyer, who studied design at Parsons. "We sell affordable exotic and traditional items that can be seamlessly incorporated into these homes, updating and refreshing existing collections." William-Wayne accessories range from Chinese rattan wedding chests to Venetian-inspired mirrored boxes and hand-embroidered linen pillows decorated with the ancient tree of life pattern. Their shops demonstrate the many ways to display accessories in the home, and are a real joy to visit. Many William-Wayne products, including furniture and antiques, can be seen on the company's website. Retail. **Call 800-318-3435 or visit www.william-wayne.com.**

**SKYSCRAPER AND DECO DELUXE II**
Skyscraper and sister store Deco Deluxe II offer a huge selection of vintage items, most from the 1930s to 1950s. Their Art Deco products hail from a wide variety of different countries and designers, and include everything from candelabras, clocks and fireplace accessories to furniture and light fixtures. Owner Sandi Berman brings her items to antique and modernist fairs focusing on 20th-century design. (Show dates are listed on the company website.) While stock is ever-changing, you can call to request certain pieces or request searches for items. Her wares have an unparalleled beauty: Recent finds include a sleek, silver-plated box, wrought-iron wall panels and skyscraper-inspired cologne bottles, all from 1930s France. Retail. **Call 212-588-0644 (Skyscraper) or 212-249-5066 (Deco Deluxe II) or visit www.skyscraperny.com.**

**CAROLE STUPELL**
Considered by some to be the country's finest home accessories store, Carole Stupell carries a dizzying array of silver, crystal, ceramics and more. The nearly 2,000-square-foot Manhattan venue is overflowing with high-end European and American goods, from vases to candlesticks and picture frames, with some dating back to the 1940s and still in the original packaging. (Rather fittingly, the store's founder is said to have created the first bridal registry, back in the early 1930s.) The company also offers a replacement service for many of the tabletop patterns that it has sold over the past 75 years. Retail. **Call 212-260-3100.**

**J. POCKER & SONS**
For over 75 years, family-run J. Pocker & Sons has been providing custom framing for the New York area. The company also sells unframed art and about 50 stock matted and framed prints, featuring everything from sporting dogs to topography maps. Designers like to use J. Pocker's moldings to add an antique touch to their clients' mirrors and photograph frames. The company recently launched a website, and has retail locations dotted throughout New York and Connecticut, as well as a To the Trade showroom in Manhattan. From French to Spanish and Oriental, there's a frame for every décor. Retail and To the Trade. **Call 800-443-3116 or visit www.dir-dd.com/jpocker_framing.html.**

**LYONS LTD. ANTIQUE PRINTS** 5, 6
For the past several decades, Lyons Ltd. has made a name for itself selling original antique etchings, engravings and lithographs dating from 1490 to 1920. Its sheer variety keeps shoppers spellbound: flower and fruit prints from the 18th and 19th centuries, architectural prints from the time of Columbus, and bird illustrations that include hand-colored stone lithographs from John James Audubon's *Birds of America* (1841 and 1848 editions). Lyons also carries maps and other types of works on paper, including portraits, Japanese woodblocks and lithographed posters. Prints are generally documented, and sent "on approval" to clients. They also come with a lifetime exchange privilege. Items can be viewed at the company's Palo Alto showroom, or at various print shows (check the website for details). Retail. **Call 800-596-6758 or visit www.lyonsltdantiqueprints.com.**

Ridless chose a neoclassic backdrop for his apartment's antiques and upholstered furniture. A large, darkly stained antique drafting table grounds the far end of the room.

RANDY RIDLESS

CHAPTER 11

# TRADITIONAL REDEFINED

Randy Ridless has been fascinated by interior design for as long as he can remember. As a child, he created sophisticated room schemes in discarded shoeboxes, filling them with scraps of textile and wallpaper and fashioning furniture from bits of cardboard. Encouraged by his artistic family, he then began to draw and execute model fantasy rooms, many of which were not so different (at least conceptually) from the showhouse rooms he creates today. By the age 22, Ridless had a degree in industrial design from the prestigious Rhode Island School of Design. He has been practicing the craft ever since.

Ridless currently splits his time between residential and commercial jobs, with the latter generating more press. He is the man behind Burberry's successful brand redesign of 2000, which has given the 150-year-old English company a more youthful, less stodgy appeal without compromising its historical character. He also recently finished updating the first two floors of Manhattan's sophisticated Bergdorf-Goodman store. Because of his retail design experience, Ridless is known as the designer to call when you need to make over staid, traditional spaces, motifs or brands.

In 1999, after spending 15 years in retail store design—including stints at Macy's and Saks Fifth Avenue—and two years in residential design (with David Easton), Ridless decided to open his own residential business with Beth Martell, now vice president. The projects shown here include two of his own apartments and two of his firm's showhouse rooms.

The sisal rug in this formal living room makes its antiques and other precious decorative elements look less formal and more inviting.

*"There is a* **visual tension** *created when old is placed against new. The traditional accents add* **character** *and* **warmth** *to the modern space while the modern elements make the antiques look* **less serious."**

## Design Influences

For his former apartment, located in the Manhattan's Gramercy neighborhood, Ridless wanted to create an "Elsie de Wolfe" mood. De Wolfe is credited (or perhaps more accurately, credited herself) with being the first interior designer. Her design style, which emphasized light spaces, was a reaction to the excessive decoration of 19th-century Victorian homes. When she began her career, in the early 1900s, architecture and design were being greatly affected by the rapid growth of industrialization and the mass production of decorative elements. Architectural details, furniture and accessories had suddenly become inexpensive and widely available, and homes, in turn, became architecturally overbearing, overwhelmingly patterned and uniformly dark. De Wolfe was one of the first to reject this uniform clutter and darkness. She dismissed the intricate textiles, discarded the bric-a-brac dominating shelving and painted dark moldings and furniture bright white.

"I love her philosophy of a lighter, fresher palette," Ridless says. "She removed the pretension from grand spaces and created intimate ones that referenced history. Like de Wolfe, I'm inspired by period rooms—I admire their character and warmth. But when I design, I see it as a game. I need to figure out how to make period styles youthful and approachable."

Ridless completed the Gramercy apartment a decade ago. To give it a fresh look, he combined complementary design styles from the 18th and 19th century, such as Sweden's Gustavian, and France's Louis the XVI and Directoire—all of which had pleasant, muted color schemes and restrained furniture features (especially when compared to their predecessors).

Ridless started by tearing out the apartment's sheetrock,

This detail of Ridless' former living room shows how complex patterns—whether plaid, checkered, Greek key pattern, sisal or distressed paint—can work together. The secret lies in choosing complementary tones.

DESIGNER TIPS

**Keep Traditional Spaces Light and Uncluttered:** If you use light tones and dismiss clutter, traditional spaces will be perceived as youthful and vibrant.

**Pattern Judiciously:** Limit pattern to one aspect of a room. Choose patterned rugs, walls or upholstery, but leave the other elements plain. Rooms with strict, limited patterns look clean and orderly. Various textures can be used to decorate the rest of the space for additional interest.

**Update Antiques:** Upholster old furniture with solid fabrics or animal skins to make them seem more fashionable and less precious.

**Use Modern Elements:** Consider straw, bamboo and rattan pieces, which take the edge off formal spaces and make them seem more inviting.

In his bedroom, Ridless uses patterns on everything but the bed. Striped, floral and checked patterns work well together because of their complementary tones and placement. If a pattern had been used on the bed, the room's design would have been overbearing.

rebuilding the walls with old world plaster. He then added classic architectural elements, including large, simply designed moldings, decorative pilasters and radiator cabinets. The apartment's color palette was limited to straw, cream and yellow, with blue accents.

For furniture, the designer generally chose carved Swedish and French antiques with pale, sometimes weathered finishes. Pattern in the living room is limited to the upholstered pieces; a simple sisal rug and silk curtains with a subtle check gently blend with the room's creamy yellow walls. The walls of the bedroom were upholstered in a stripe, and its carpet had a pattern, but the bed was simply covered in a cream-colored cotton matelassé.

Ridless' admiration for another great 20th-century designer, Billy Baldwin, was equally evident in his plan for the apartment. Like de Wolfe, Baldwin was greatly influenced by French design, but he favored contemporary styles. And while he loved luxury, he disdained a conspicuously "rich" look. He is remembered for designing classically inspired spaces, lightening them with straw, rattan and bamboo.

Baldwin limited his color palette, often working tone-on-tone. "I admire his strict color choices," Ridless says. "It gave his rooms a sense of purity. Additionally, he would color block, meaning he would upholster antiques in solid colors and textures as a way to unify them and give them a less pretentious look."

In Ridless' former apartment, Baldwin's influence could be seen in the controlled furniture layout and tabletop design, the limited placement of pattern and the addition of a sisal carpet to the living room. "Baldwin gave new clarity to historically inspired rooms by tightly editing them," Ridless notes. "He limited color, pattern and decorative accessories. His rooms were clean and strong."

Ridless' current apartment merges the old and new. Antiques, reproductions and a textured cowhide rug add character and warmth, creating a playful balance between forms and shapes.

## A Distinctive Style

Ridless furnished his current apartment with antique furniture and pieces he designed himself. Upholstered in solid textiles and leather, and unified by their fixed color palette—chocolate, saddle browns and white—they formed a striking silhouette against the backdrop of the modern architecture that surrounded them.

The designer wanted the apartment's architectural shell to be simple, but he didn't want it to be completely bare. "The apartment was basically a white box," he remembers. "The first thing I planned to do was to create a focal point, installing a built-in bookcase and filling it with my design books." Since Ridless consults his books frequently, their worn appearance added considerable character to the room. A collection of (largely) modern arwork also provided a nice contrast to the antique furniture.

"There is visual tension created when old is placed against new," Ridless explains. "The traditional accents add character and warmth to the modern space while modern elements make the antiques look less serious."

## Showhouse Rooms

In the beach-inspired showhouse room featured here, Ridless took his cues from a fictitious muse—a "sophisticated, female marine biologist." Save for its walls, the room was devoid of pattern, but full of texture. "At this point, I like to limit patterns to one aspect of a room," Ridless says. "Here, the pattern was on the walls, but in another setting, it could have been on the floor, or on the upholstery. A limited pattern gives the eye something to focus on, but doesn't overwhelm the viewer. Keeping pattern to a minimum makes rooms appear more youthful."

Working with a limited color scheme, Ridless painted the floors and ceiling white, and chose cotton upholstery and sheer window treatments. He laid down a sisal area rug and installed straw Roman shades beneath the sheers. He then

This built-in bookcase adds visual interest to Ridless' clean, white architectural shell. The shelves are filled with an extensive collection of well-worn design books, which add pattern and character.

This enchanting wall pattern, perfect for a beach house guestroom, was inspired by an 18th-century Japanese print. Restricting the pattern to the wall makes its impact stronger.

The interplay of the wall panels' motifs works well in this eclectically designed room. The color palette—brown and white, with dashes of pink—suggests tradition, but with doses of original, daring thought.

**Use Silhouette Techniques:** Furniture takes on a scultpural silhouette when placed against a backdrop of simple, modern architecture.

**Create Positive Tension:** Pairing modern art with antique furniture creates positive tension. The art makes the antiques look less serious, while the antiques make the modern art look less severe.

**Display Your Books:** Bookcases filled with your favorite, everyday books (rather than leather-bound versions) give rooms character and a sense of informality.

**Enlarge Prints and Try Unique Combinations:** When traditional motifs are enlarged, they retain their enchanting familiarity yet become novel additions to rooms. You might also try combining an eclectic array of historic motifs to form a new pattern. They will create unexpected, yet inviting designs.

filled the space with furniture his firm designed. The only real antique-looking object in the room was a Venetian mirror.

To create the patterned wall covering, Ridless combed through 18th-century Japanese prints, enlarging them to see how their finer details would appear on a bigger scale. He chose one print to inspire his design, and had it hand-painted on bark paper, for added texture. "The original print was 15 by 20 inches," Ridless recalls. "By blowing up its details, they become exaggerated, overscaled and new."

Ridless frequently enlarges antique prints, design motifs and other patterns when looking for inspiration. To create a design for the Burberry stores, he cleverly enlarged its trademark red, camel, black and white plaid to various scales, which transformed it into a series of abstract grids These grids were then placed throughout the company's stores, establishing a unified design scheme.

For the 2000 Kips Bay Decorator Showhouse, in Manhattan, Ridless created a study inspired by the Metropolitan Museum of Art's French Crillon Room. Featuring a strict palette of brown and beige (the signature Billy Baldwin combination), it was delightfully punched up with doses of hot pink. But the most interesting aspect of the room was its lacquered wall panels, which Ridless says were inspired by, African textiles, a Matisse painting, the Villa Kryos and Japanese lacquerware. The panels were bordered by rich, cream-colored walls, suggestive of Elsie de Wolfe's early predilection for dark walls with bright white trim. With their eclectic patterns, the panels added an element of the unexpected to the room.

Ridless, like many of his peers, continues to refine and redefine his decorative style. He began by taking cues from his design idols, but has since gone on to develop his own signature look—in both retail and residential spaces.

Thank goodness his family encouraged him to play with shoeboxes.

This showhouse room would have been just another attractive, well-appointed space, if not for the unexpected, hand-painted brown and gold wall panels, which are highlighted by strong moldings in contrasting white.

# PLUMBING

1.

2.

*The residential bathroom has been completely reinvigorated over the last decade. From a design perspective, it is now as important as any other public room in the house, and is decorated accordingly. To appeal to customers who want historically inspired bathrooms, plumbing manufacturers look back to the grand fittings and fixtures of yesteryear, as well as to items that predate the 19th-century indoor bathroom. (In plumbing parlance, "fixtures" are porcelain pieces; "fittings" are hardware.) The following are designers' favorite sources for antique and vintage-style plumbing and tiles, with prices that range from affordable to expensive. For more information on refurbished plumbing, see the section on architectural salvage.*

**ARTISANS: DEEDEE GUNDBERG, ANN SACKS** 1, 2

Just a decade ago, DeeDee Gundberg was a brand-new college graduate with a degree in historic preservation from Roger Williams University and a job answering phones at Ann Sacks. Today, she is the company's design director, in charge of tile and stone. Two of her newest ceramic bathroom tile collections are Blue Hour and Veranda: "Both are inspired by architectural details," she says from the company's corporate office in Portland, OR. "Because of my background in historical preservation, my shelves are lined with books about historic styles. I chose architectural elements from various periods that I thought would translate well into tile." The Art Deco-inspired Blue Hour, which echoes the shade of an evening sky, is named after the time of day the French consider most romantic. Veranda is based on window and door molding details, including the basket weaves and bamboo patterns seen on traditional Victorian brownstones. It is so named because it has the light, airy look of wicker furniture one might find on a veranda. "My inspiration for these lines came from books, but tile sources really come from everywhere," Gundberg explains. "I've come to believe that no design is truly original."

That may be true, but it takes considerable talent to successfully update and translate traditional motifs with such consistency. In addition to over 200 collections of ceramic and stone tile, Ann Sacks carries bathroom fittings, fixtures and accessories, on view at 17 U.S. showrooms and through 20 additional retailers. The company is owned by Kohler. For more information on this source, see the section on flooring. Retail. **Call 800-278-8453 or visit www.annsacks.com.**

3.

**COMPANY IN FOCUS: WATERWORKS** 4, 5

Consistently at the top of interior design magazines' "Best-Of" lists, the 25-year-old Waterworks has played a major role in revolutionizing bathroom design. Founders Barbara and Robert Sallick and their son Peter have made it their goal to bring elegance and craftsmanship back to the American bath, and their Danbury, CT, company accordingly offers top-shelf fittings, fixtures, lighting and tile. Inspiration comes from old world sources, including grand, traditional European hotels, luxury ocean liners, 19th-century French interiors and French and English Art Deco design. The elegantly rounded forms of the Easton collection were inspired by 1920s Edwardian bathroom fittings, while the Boulevard collection combines vintage glamour and romance to produce crystal washstand and shower accents, a mirrored medicine cabinet, gray-and-black mosaic wall tiles, and a checkered marble floor. The French-inspired Amélie collection is equally feminine, but more low-key, while the Elsa, Beacon and Waterworks Highgate lines are aimed at those with a limited budget. Two of Waterworks' most popular collections are designer Thomas O'Brien's Aero and Aero Retro, which offer classic looks with a contemporary edge; O'Brien modeled his pieces after a host of unusual sources, including 19th-century telescope fittings and 18th-century furniture decorations. The company has dozens of U.S. stores, a catalog and a website. Retail. **Call 800-899-6757 or visit www.waterworks.com.**

4.

5.

**P.E. GUERIN** 3

Family-run P.E. Guerin has been manufacturing high-end hardware—including plumbing fittings—since the mid-19th-century. A pioneer in the field of artistic metalwork, it offers a wide range of period and vintage faucets, showerheads and related accessories. The selection is diverse, to say the least: The Scallop collection's strong, distinct lines draw from English Gothic; ornamental Acanthus is inspired by the Louis XVI period; Ritz builds on the strong, masculine forms of the Edwardian era; and New World's rounded, unusual forms are Bauhaus in origin. Custom work makes up the bulk of Guerin's business; stock items are largely made of solid brass and steel, with 20 stock and custom finishes. The company has five U.S. showrooms, another in Puerto Rico, and a website. For more information on this source, see the section on hardware. To the Trade. **Call 212-243-5270 or visit www.peguerin.com.**

6.

**ARTISTIC TILE**
Artistic Tile carries over 100 collections made from stone, porcelain, ceramic, glass, metal, cement, leather and cork. Some of its lines are based on ancient patterns that founder Nancy Epstein spots on scouting trips to places such as the Middle East, Africa, Europe and Mexico. Among her newer collections are Italian Akros marble tiles and Tunisian limestone mosaics—both perfect for bathrooms. Akros is made using the 16th-century Aquaforte technique, which involves the use of acid to etch pattern into marble. The Tunisian limestone mosaics are reproductions and inspired by versions of documentary patterns Epstein discovered in Africa, including those found on tile still clinging to ruins. Artistic Tile also carries vessel, drop-in and farmhouse sinks, and has five U.S. showrooms. Products are also sold at another 100+ locations throughout the country, and by catalog. For more information about this source, see the section on flooring. Retail and To the Trade. **Call 800-260-8646 or visit www.artistictile.com.**

**HERBEAU** 6 (page 169)
Herbeau was founded in France over 150 years ago, just as plumbing began its civilized move inside. The family-run company is now based in Naples, FL, where it sells items based on its own plumbing fixture and fitting designs from 1857 to the 1950s. The delightful Pompadour faucet, a tribute to Louis XIV and his mistress, Madame de Pompadour, features a gargoyle over the spout, a nod to the Château of Versailles' rain gutters. A petite Arabesque powder room set and Royale mirror boast the sensuous lines of Art Nouveau, while the company's newly reintroduced Minark line echoes the elegant, streamlined forms of Art Deco. Herbeau also carries a line of hand-painted sinks, which are decorated with traditional French floral patterns. Products are sold through 300+ U.S. dealers and by catalog. Retail. **Call 239-417-5368 or visit www.herbeau.com.**

**LEFROY BROOKS** 2
Lefroy Brooks manufactures shower systems, showerheads, faucets, accessories, light fixtures and "chinaware" (tubs, sinks and commodes). Based in England, it reveres an old world approach. In the case of its brass faucets, for example, all of the casting, polishing and assembly is done by hand. An Edwardian line of chinaware remains unchanged since it was first introduced in 1923, while the Lissa Doon collection (named after a Scottish castle) was inspired by 19th-century fixtures and fittings. Generally, the company's fittings are divided into three categories: Edwardian, Empire and Liberty. The streamlined Edwardian collection mimics bathroom hardware from the early 20th-century reign of Edward VII, while Empire echoes the fittings installed on Victorian ocean liners and Liberty recalls the 1920s French-style bathrooms of World War I's Liberté period. Two impressive new collections are Edwardian 1900s Black and Art Deco 1930s Mackintosh. All of Brooks' products have a timeless quality to them, which makes them appear simultaneously old-fashioned and modern. Contact the company for a list of U.S. dealers; a catalog and website are also available. Retail. **Call 212-226-2242 or visit www.lefroybrooks.com.**

**URBAN ARCHEOLOGY** 3
Gil Shapiro founded Urban Archaeology as a salvage company in the 1980s. Today, the Manhattan-based firm still sells salvage, but its main business is high-end antiques and vintage reproductions, with a focus on items dating back to the 19th century. Current products include bath fixtures, stone and ceramic tiles, and accessories, including a curvaceous Victorian washstand carved from white Carrara, a sleek Lenox medicine cabinet based on a salvaged design from the early 20th-century, and a marble bathtub that resembles a stylized trough. The firm's tiles hail from 50 American manufacturers, and range from historic to rustic and contemporary. Its multidimensional, crackled-glass tiles come in a variety of classic styles, while a French Metro line reproduces those made for the restoration of the Paris subway. "Custom orders are welcomed, and frequently act as inspiration for new products," Shapiro says. Urban Archaeology has four East Coast showrooms and 90 U.S. and Canadian distributors. For more information on this source, see the section on light fixtures. Retail and To the Trade. **Call 212-431-4646 or visit www.urbanarchaeology.com.**

**KALLISTA**
Kallista offers several lines of traditionally inspired plumbing fixtures and fittings. Most prominently, it carries pieces by noted American interior designers Barbara Barry and Michael Smith, a series of painted basins (including two from Tracey Porter) and a Retro Collection based on its founder's original, English-style plumbing designs. The Barbara Barry collection consists of three lines—Java Wood, White Wood and Glamour. Java Wood is an elegant combination of mahogany, Carrara

marble and brushed nickel, while White Wood has a more rustic appeal and the mirrored Glamour collection recalls Hollywood's early days. Michael Smith also has three plumbing collections—For Town, For Country and For Loft— whose titles clearly define their styles. Inspired by Art Deco and other designs from the 1930s and '40s, they feature streamlined forms that speak to both female and male sensibilities. On the opposite end of the spectrum, Kallista's painted lavatory basins from Tracey Porter recall a simpler time, with fanciful floral motifs perfect for a country home. Kallista is owned by Kohler. Retail. **Call 888-452-5547 or visit www.kallistainc.com.**

**RENAISSANCE TILE AND BATH**

Designers praise Renaissance Tile and Bath for its variety of fittings, fixtures and tiles, its knowledgeable staff and its outstanding customer service. Founded in 1991 by David O'Neil and architect Randy Ruppel, it was originally a design studio that made high-end tile. But the Atlanta-based company soon expanded, and now sells upscale tile and bath items, including brands mentioned in this chapter and a customized O'Neil Ruppel line. The company still specializes in tile: Its stone mosaics come in classic and blended patterns (for a more contemporary take on the ancient), while a rustic collection handcrafted in Bali uses an old sand-casting technique to create a rough, antiqued surface. "We are the industry's Saks Fifth Avenue," O'Neil says. "We carry every available high-end line." Renaissance has four U.S. showrooms, a catalog and a company website. Retail. **Call 800-275-1822 or visit www.renaissancetileandbath.com.**

**KOHLER** 1

Kohler has been a respected name in the plumbing industry for over 120 years. The Wisconsin-based company sells complete lines of reasonably priced plumbing for the bathroom, including vintage styles that can be bought as "suites", allowing for easy coordination. One collection with considerable appeal is the Memoirs Suite: Its Classic design features soft, rounded details resembling traditional moldings, while its Stately design boasts clean, crisp, masculine lines. The Kathryn Suite is a revival of Kohler's Art Deco fixtures and fittings, as first seen in a 1929 exhibit at New York's Metropolitan Museum of Art. Sleek and sophisticated, the fixtures currently come in white or black. Products are available in showrooms across the country, and by catalog; the company's website offers a design planner. Kohler is the parent company of the higher-end Kallista and Ann Sacks brands, also mentioned in this chapter. Retail. **Call 800-456-4537 or visit www.kohler.com.**

1.

2.

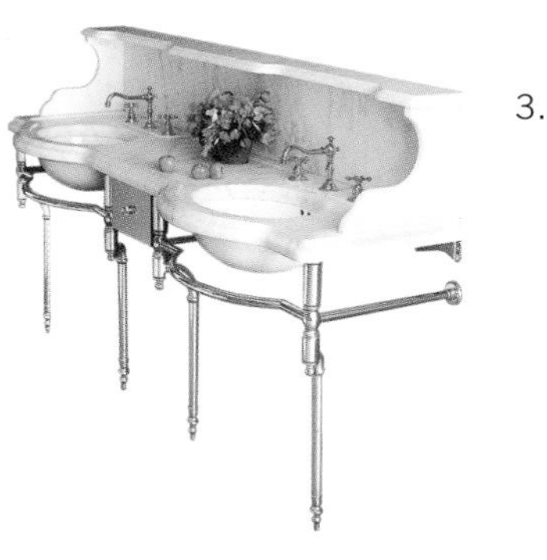

3.

PETER CHU

CHAPTER 12

# EASTERN INFLUENCE

Even though brothers Peter and David Chu left Tapei as young boys more than 35 years ago, the two still maintain strong ties to their Eastern roots—and to each other. Peter, an architect and interior designer, has designed Nautica stores for brother David, the company's founder, as well as Coach stores, an awarding winning America Café and model apartments for Trump Plaza. He has also been involved with historic restorations in Manhattan, including the University Club, which was originally designed by McKim, Mead and White. David, meanwhile, is the CEO of Nautica and a designer for the company, which, in addition to its clothing and related accessories business, has a home collection and a line of furniture manufactured by Lexington.

Their individual resumés are impressive, but the brothers are even more formidable when they work together. This chapter features the design of David's Upper East Side penthouse, to which he and his family recently moved at wife Gina's bequest, from their Georgian style suburban home. To plan the new apartment, David called on the services of his younger brother, who runs the firm Chu/Petterson with *his* wife, Theresa.

**Opposite:** The apartment introduces its Asian theme at the front door, using Ming hunting chairs and an antique Buddha.

## A Joint Venture

For their third collaboration, each brother took a specific role in the design of the sprawling, 7,000-square-foot penthouse. David guided the overall look, purchasing much of the furniture, artwork, artifacts and accessories, while Peter planned the architectural details, wall finishes and window treatments. David wanted the penthouse to reflect his personality, which he calls a fusion of Asian and American influences. "In the end, it represented a meeting point between East and West," Peter recalls. "We placed Asian antiques and artifacts against a classic, largely Western backdrop."

The space that would become David's future home was actually part of a former hotel. "Given that we were dealing with raw space, our first step was to design the most basic components," Peter explains. "David had bought the top two floors of the building and a portion of the roof, which allowed for more indoor space, a terrace and a garden. We had to lay out the rooms and determine their flow."

The apartment would require a clear division between public and private spaces, as David would be using it to

This living room demonstrates how to give a new space a sense of history in a clean, uncluttered way. Its walls serve as a muted backdrop for the family's collection of antiques, reproductions and artifacts.

*"I love to execute a classic idea or concept in an* **unexpected** *way. In the case of the* **furniture** *I designed, I chose* **unusual materials** *or woods that aren't available in the East. By doing so, the ordinary becomes* **extraordinary."**

entertain clients and colleagues. The brothers decided that the public rooms would be located on the top floor, with easy access to both the rooftop terrace and the bottom floor's private rooms.

It was equally important for the apartment to be tranquil and uncluttered. "David liked the calm feeling he got when going to the suburbs," his brother remembers. "If he was going to move into the city, he needed his apartment to be clean, classic and serene."

The Chus opted to give the penthouse an understated architectural shell, using minimal moldings and wall finishes and choosing window treatments in neutral colors. This novel

In this large living room, Peter Chu created two conversation areas, one centered around the fireplace and the other located near the window. The cozy seating inspires intimate gatherings.

DESIGNER TIPS

**Design For Your Needs:** The first step to planning a new interior is determining a layout that will best suit your family. Next, plan the size of the rooms, taking into account who will use them and how much they will be used, and making sure there is a natural flow between the public rooms. The private rooms should be clustered in their own space.

**Develop a Theme:** A clear concept should guide your design. In David Chu's apartment, the theme was East meets West. The brothers determined which elements would be Eastern and which Western before they even started.

**Limit Architectural Details:** A contemporary approach to designing a new space with old world charm is to use minimal architectural details painted in a neutral color scheme. To flesh out the simple backdrop, fill in the room with antiques, antique reproductions and artifacts. The furniture and objects give the room its character and look sculptural against the muted background.

**Start Simple and Blend:** To create a flat-looking canvas as the backdrop for your furniture, pick simple moldings and minimal window treatments that blend into the walls.

**Diversify Your Furnishings:** To create an interesting collection of one style of furniture, gather furniture from different time periods in that style. Then follow the same idea with your art and artifacts. Rooms full of furniture and art from one style and one period translate as staid period rooms.

approach to old world design would turn the pared-down shell into a strong, museum-like background for the room's historical contents.

With a nod to his family's origins, Peter installed a crown and base molding on the apartment's walls, but left its windows and doors untrimmed. "In the East, exterior windows and doors tend to be very simple, with few adornments," Peter explains. "We wanted to treat David's doors and windows the same way, with a simplicity that would serve our overall purpose."

The architect and interior designer had an equally inventive solution for disguing obtrusive structural beams in the living room. "If we had simply filled them in, the ceiling would have appeared very low and heavy, given the scale of the room," Peter says. "Instead, we used them to create a ceiling pattern, covered them in gypsum board and added a nice finish." With their straight, modern, discreet lines, the built-ins now resmeble a coffered ceiling.

"The majority of the architectural details in our home are very classic, but with a modern edge," David recalls. "They are very clean and unobtrusive. I love to distill classic design down to its essence—it becomes modern."

The fashion designer insisted on giving his apartment a neutral background, with linen-colored walls and white, painted ceilings. All of the walls bore similar tones, but Peter Chu had them finished in different ways to add interest and subtly distinguish them from one another. Among the finishes he used were lacquer,

Peter used mahogany to create these built-in bookshelves. The dark, rich wood adds warmth to the space and creates interest by contrasting with the white walls.

Old meets new: A roof ornament from a Thai temple sits in front of a painting by contemporary Dutch artist, Jan Grotenbreg. Ching Dynasty porcelains perch atop Asian blackwood pedestals.

custom painting and fabric-backed wallpaper. The living room walls were covered in cream-colored silk, while in the adjoining library, the walls are finished in a white matte lacquer.

"The wall treatments are beautiful but understated," Peter says. "They added another level of refinement and character to the apartment."

So, too, did Roman window treatments, made from lined and unlined silk. When pulled down, the luxurious, flat shades almost seemed to blend into the walls. "We chose Asian-inspired window treatments," Peter recalls. "But we didn't line the ones in the public rooms, because we wanted them to resmble rice paper. Now, when the sun shines through the silk, the treatments glow, which adds more interest to the room—albeit in a subtle way."

To ground the apartment's neutrally colored rooms, the brothers gave most of them ebony-stained wood floors. (Limestone and granite were also used.) They then brought in furniture and textiles to add warmth and a distinctive Asian look. David avidly collects Eastern antiques—many of which he buys in Europe or Asia—and decided to fill his space with an eclectic collection of Asian furniture and artifacts.

## Unique Perspectives on Asian-Inspired Design

"A lot of Asian furniture and artifacts are still not appreciated in the West," Peter says. "You tend to see the same pieces over and over again, such as the classic Ming chair. It is the more unusual pieces that sets David's apartment apart from others that are Asian-inspired."

Among the elder Chu's more curious items are his Ming hunting chairs and an 18th-century black, lacquered table with an openwork base, both located in the apartment's foyer. In the living room, there is a beautifully proportioned, antique Monk's bed, while Gina's office boasts a sculptural

**Top:** David Chu designed this large table, which anchors the dining room. He also created the ceiling fixture, a modern interpretation of a Japanese shoji screen.

**Opposite, bottom:** Translucent glass blocks a view of the apartment's staircase while still allowing light to filter in from the roof. An Eastern-influenced table creates an interesting juxtaposition of old and new.

**Above:** An antique Asian screen, two traditional Chinese horseshoe arm-chairs and a 1,000-plus year-old Chinese artifact lend this master bedroom a subtle Eastern flavor. They are nicely balanced by a Christian Liagre chest (which David found in Paris) and a Patrick Naggar chaise lounge from Ralph Pucci.

Clean, simple, classic lines define this limestone and mahogany master bath. Its shape and form sets an uncomplicated, meditative tone.

DESIGNER TIPS

**Create Asian-Inspired Window Treatments:** To create the look of traditional Asian rice paper window treatments, have shades made from unlined white or linen-colored silk. They will slightly filter the light coming into your home and give rooms an intriguing glow.

**Reinterpret Classic Ideas:** Execute an old idea or concept in an unexpected way, using a novel material or rare wood. For example, have a classic Asian pedestal table fashioned out of iron or brass. This breaths new life into the commonplace while retaining important historical references.

**Make It Light and Airy:** Dark floors ground rooms. Light floors in light rooms allow furniture to float.

**Create More Than One Seating Area:** In a large living room, use seats and sofas to break up the space. One grouping could be focused on the fireplace, another, on a window. Separate seating areas make the room feel cozy and inspire intimate gatherings. They're perfect for both entertaining and hanging out with the family.

**Incorporate Structural Beams:** If you have structural beams and low ceiling heights, consider using the beams to make a coffered pattern. Walling them in would make the room appear smaller.

antique Asian wardrobe. 'Some of my favorite pieces are the reconditioned antiques, made from rare woods such as Huanghuali (yellow rosewood) and Zitan (purple sandalwood)," says Peter.

If the Chus couldn't find an item they wanted, they had it custom made, with a specificaly Eastern flavor. David designed two openwork desks, for example, that reinterpretated Ming tables. "I love to execute a classic idea or concept in an unexpected way," he says. "In the case of the furniture I designed, I chose unusual materials or woods that aren't available in the East. By doing so, the ordinary becomes extraordinary."

David also designed some of his apartment's upholstered furniture and light fixtures. Soafas he created for the living room are Eastern by design, with straight lines and rectangular shapes. The dining room ceiling fixture, made out of wood and paper, was inspired by Japanese shoji screens.

To accessorize his new home, David chose stone and porcelain pieces, paintings and photographs by Eastern artists. "I am in awe of some of the Chinese sculpture in our home," he says. "Our Tang dynasty horse was created by someone 2,000 years ago. It's amazing. Good design is ageless. Pieces from different periods and eras blend harmoniously when they share good design."

And that is the secret to the beauty of this apartment. Good design is ageless, whether found in a modern interpretation of a classic coffered ceiling, or a 2,000-year-old artifact. When paired together, such items create a character-rich environment that is both old-world and fashionable. What could be better?

The daybed, upholstered in green bouclé fabric, is from the Nautica Home collection, by Lexington. It looks stunning against an antique Asian wardrobe and a lined, silk Roman shades.

# TRADE TIPS

1.

2.

3.

## DESIGNER TIPS: AVOIDING PREDICTABILITY IN TRADITIONAL INTERIORS

**BY ELLEN S. FISHER, ASID** 1

DESIGNER; ASSOC DEAN, NY SCHOOL OF INTERIOR DESIGN

**Traditional interiors often seem formal and somber, but even a contemporary room can be uncomfortable if people are afraid to sit on the sofa because it looks too "precious." Be playful with your design and your spaces will also look fresh and unexpected. Here's how:**

**1. Play with scale and proportion:** Many traditional interiors are feminine, flowery and patterned, with delicately scaled furniture, or masculine and heavy-looking, with massive furniture and classical detailing. Mix it up: Use a large, comfortable sofa or large-scale floral or plaid in a feminine, light-filled room, or choose more tailored, light furniture for a traditionally masculine environment. Both can be lovely.

**2. Play with color:** Using color in non-traditional ways while maintaining the formal "bones" of a room adds freshness. The great decorator Billy Baldwin was famous for his living room, which featured lacquered brown walls and cream accents. And the all-red rooms he created for Diana Vreeland live on in design history. In these rooms, the furniture was considered transitional, but was arranged traditionally. Color was used to create excitement—the opposite of what was expected.

**3. Play without color:** Another great modern designer, Elsie de Wolfe, painted her antiques white, creating the first all-white interiors. When important surfaces and materials are white, the textures and lines of the fabrics and furnishings show as if they were sculpture. In an all-white interior, dark accents and floors create a warm and dramatic contrast.

**4. Use color generously:** Try broad swaths of saturated pastels, for example. Using robin's-egg blue on your dining chairs, or a rich Schiaparelli pink on the walls, is unexpected. And in a room with lots of natural light, try going darker than usual. A dark color creates a rich background for lighter furnishings. You can also try a rich color on the ceiling of a traditional room. Typically, the ceiling is the forgotten plane of a room, but it's the same size as the floor, and can greatly influence the overall feeling. When you encourage people to look up—and then delight them—some of the stuffiness of the traditional room goes away.

**5. Play with collections:** An unexpected collection enchants. One of my clients collected bottles of hot sauce from all over the world, which made for a perfect display in a custom-made cabinet in the kitchen and great room area. The cabinet was the traditional cherry, with an antiqued, painted finish, but the collection was whimsical and humorous.

**6. Play with lighting:** Recessed lighting fixtures have improved so much that there is no reason to avoid using them in a traditional interior. Some fixtures are so small, they are practically unnoticeable. But the quality and color of the light itself has gotten better. No historical interior has been able to escape a certain dimness, but the new lighting, when used with decorative table lamps, chandeliers and sconces, gives a lovely, warm, white scintillation to a room filled with beautiful fabrics and architectural materials. It makes jewels sparkle and people look beautiful!

**7. Play with furniture arrangements:** Dare to ignore the fireplace. Go ahead—what is a fireplace anyway? Unless there is a fire blazing, a fireplace, though beautiful, is static and lifeless. A good furniture arrangement should provide something active for a seated person to look at from every location, whether it's light glittering off water or filtering through leaves, or an activity in an adjacent area—say, people playing at a game table. It is predictable to center a traditional seating area around a fireplace. If you act as if the fireplace was simply part of the wall, the room becomes more dynamic and people-centered.

Another way to render a formal room unpredictable is to allow some seating that encourages or anticipates informal behavior. For instance, large floor pillows practically beckon guests to sit on the floor. A chaise with an ottoman gives off a relaxed air, as does an oversized "chair-and-a-half." Mixing in unusual pieces, such as African low stools or Asian tables, also adds interest.

**8. Play with window treatments:** What does someone say when they want to change a serious mood? Lighten up! The same applies to the windows of a traditional interior. Using heavy, formal valances and lambrequins in a traditional room give the space a fusty, restrictive air. Install a beautiful rod and lightweight curtains instead. One year, in a top-tier designer showhouse, a decorator used a tree branch as a curtain rod, and hung airy, white sheers accented with seashell fringe from it. The look was imaginative and new.

**9. Play with fabrics:** Angelo Donghia was the first to use menswear fabrics for upholstery. In the '70s, he introduced gray flannel, navy pinstripes, oxford cloth and serape cottons to formal rooms, where he used them to adorn simple slipper chairs and sectional sofas. While others continue to do this for modern interiors, the idea can be successfully applied to traditional rooms, where it provides just the right note of unpredictability. Cashmere woolens, terry cloth, kidskin, rugby stripes, cotton broadcloth in all colors—these familiar fabrics evoke a feeling of comfort in an interior environment.

**10. Play with technology:** After spending thousands on a high-tech stereo or a flat-screen television, do you really want to hide it? For years, many traditional living spaces have included a huge cabinet, which hid an equally huge television and stereo system. This type of cabinetry will soon be obsolete as electronics become smaller and less obtrusive. A hard-and-fast rule has been that in a traditional interior, the entertainment system should never be visible. The challenge now is: How do you hide modern equipment in a new way? When it comes to traditional rooms, why not display a flat-screen television in a traditional frame? Now that would truly be unpredictable!

## COMPANY IN FOCUS: DESIGNER PREVIEWS 2, 3

If you want to work with an interior designer but find the idea of hiring one as daunting as selecting a financial planner, try a client-to-designer matchmaking service. Karen Fisher, founder of Manhattan's Designer Previews, is frequently referred to as a "decorating psychologist", a nod to her talent for finding just the right designer to meet her clients' needs. (Unlike head shrinks, Fisher offers her expertise for a flat fee of $100.)

This "matchmaker" meets clients in her Manhattan office, or uses the Internet to chat with them and send images. Fisher shows each client a slideshow of interior spaces—what she calls a "designer Rorschach test"—and takes careful note of their responses, adjusting the images until she determines an appropriate design style. After the slideshow, Fisher asks additional questions concerning budget and timeframe. She also tries to get a sense of the client's personality so she can suggest designers with whom they might work well. Once the evaluation is finished, Fisher suggests three possible candidates, whom the client then calls for an interview.

As a former design editor at *Women's Wear Daily* (and

numerous other magazines), Fisher knows the industry inside and out. She has been running her business since 1984, and works with over 300 top-notch designers in the New York tri-state area. Since starting her interactive Internet consultations in 2003, she has been able to sign on designers from across the country. **Call 212-777-2966 or visit www.designerpreviews.com.**

**DESIGNER TIPS: QUESTIONS TO ASK PROSPECTIVE ARCHITECTS**
**BY IRA GRANDBERG, AIA**

**When people focus too much on a firm's size and image, or whether its work has been published, they choose the wrong architects. What are really important are an architect's creativity, flexibility, versatility, problem-solving skills and personality. When interviewing prospective architects, ask the following questions:**

1. What do you enjoy about being an architect?

2. Which period home styles are cost-prohibitive to build? (Tudor-style homes, for example, are expensive to duplicate, because of the masonry work and half-timbering.)

3. How will you adapt the period style(s) we like to suit a contemporary home? (If you want a Colonial-style house, for example, ask if it will have larger windows than the original, and if rooms will be properly proportioned. What will be the interior flow?)

4. What materials will you use and what craftspeople will you hire to make our new home look as authentic as possible?

5. Will you visit the site? (It is essential that the architect see the property before designing, so that his or her plans take advantage of views, sun exposure and prevailing winds.)

6. How will you adapt the home to suit the site? (The home should meet the needs of the landscape, rather than just use it as a backdrop.)

7. Can you show me references from former clients, contractors and interior designers? (You want to make sure that the architect has had good relationships with his or her previous clients, as well as with the contractor and designer who have a large role in your project.)

8. How will you present the architectural drawings so that I can easily understand them?

9. How long it will take to design this project, and how will that time be divided? (A custom-built home can take over 1,000 hours to design.)

10. And ask the firm's partner: Will you design the house or will it be done by a staff member?

**When reviewing an architect's portfolio, ask the following specific questions to determine his or her creativity and problem-solving skills.**

11. Do you have a signature style? (If all the homes you see in the portfolio are exactly the same, you may be able to assume that your home will look similar to what you see.)

12. What were the historic references you used in designing previous homes? How did you update them to meet the needs of the homeowner and the scale of the home?

13. What were the challenges of your previous projects, and how did you solve them?

14. Also ask specific, design-oriented questions, such as, "Why did you use that style of window in the front of the house?" or "Why did you place the porch there?" and "How do these elements enrich the historical design of the home?"

**Once drawings are presented to you, ask:**

15. How do these designs meet my needs and budget? (Ask this question in regards to each room presented.)

16. How do these designs take into account the site's constraints?

17. What do you like and dislike about the designs? (If there are negative aspects, you may be able to make alterations that help the overall project.)

**Finally, ask yourself, do I like this architect? The client-architect relationship is intimate and long-lasting. If there is no rapport, chances are the working relationship will be difficult.**

1.

## BUYING TRADE ONLY WITHOUT A DESIGNER

### DESIGN PROFESSIONALS

Some large design centers offer buying services for people who are not interested in working with a designer but still want access to high-end products. "We have access to every trade showroom in country," says company director Lin Walters. "To avoid messy situations, we only work with people who are not working with designers." Design Professionals charges clients the wholesale (or "net") price, plus a 15 percent service fee. To find a similar service close to where you live, call local design centers. Design Professionals also offers a designer matchmaking service—for free **Call 212-759-6894 or visit www.ddbuilding.com.**

### IZOLLI HOME COLLECTION

Izolli sells "to the trade" items to retail consumers, with top-shelf products from Decorative Crafts, Beacon Hill, Kravet and more. The company's website provides links to a variety of manufacturers; simply note the names and numbers of items that interest you, then contact an Izolli representative by e-mail or telephone. Within a day or two, the representative will respond with a price list. If interested, you can then purchase the products directly through them. Since not all of the listed manufacturers have websites, you may want to visit their showrooms, then contact Izolli with product information. Another option is to stop by Izolli's showroom in Agoura Hills, CA, which carries a selection of the products it sells. **Call 800-772-1343 or visit www.izolli.com.**

### DECORATOR'S SECRET 1

Located just 45 minutes outside of Manhattan, the 30,000-square-foot Decorator's Secret carries trade items for as little as one-third of the retail price. Boasting over a million yards of textiles from top brands such as Carlton V, Boussac Fadini and Rose Cumming, it also features furniture from Louis Mittman, Edward Ferrell, J. Robert Scott and M2L, as well as Gracie Studios' famous hand-painted wallpaper. Over 50 percent of the company's clients are designers looking for a deal. **Call 203-323-5093 or visit www.thedecoratorssecret.com.**

## SOURCES

### THE FRANKLIN REPORT

Having trouble finding reputable upholsterers or antique refinishers in your area? Consult The Franklin Report. Designers do. First published in the late 1990s, the guide offers unbiased reports based on client reviews of home service providers, from architects to mill workers and window washers. The guides currently cover Chicago, Connecticut, Los Angeles, New York City, and Westchester, NY, and are updated yearly. **Call 866-990-9100 or visit www.franklinreport.com.**

### HOMEPORTFOLIO

The HomePortfolio website allows visitors to look through product information and images for thousands of home design items. The largest Internet database of its kind, HomePortfolio features goods from over 1,700 retailers, and even connects visitors to local shops that carry the products they want to buy. (Over 100,000 shops are listed.) Some of this book's sources can be found on the website, including Desiron (for window treatment hardware), Urban Archaeology (for light fixtures) and Brunschwig & Fils (for textiles). **Visit www.homeportfolio.com.**

### CONSIGNMENT, THRIFT AND FLEA

Even high-end designers enjoying browsing flea markets and consignment and thrift stores. The Connecticut Trading Company (located in Wilton, CT) and The Silk Purse (in New Canaan, CT), for example, offer high quality consigned antiques, accessories and more, all at reasonable prices. Thrift stores are generally known for clothing, but frequently carry donated window treatments, furniture and accessories. Shopping at consignment and thrift stores in affluent parts of the country (generally just outside major cities) guarantees high quality goods, though prices will be a bit higher than elsewhere. Planning a trip to Maine? Route One is an antique lover's paradise—and the further you get from Boston, the better the values will be. Be sure to stop by Wiscasset, ME's Marston House and Searsport, ME's Pumpkin Patch Antiques, which have an abundance of folk art, painted Colonial furniture and antique quilts. Finally, flea markets require patience and tenacity, but the rewards can be huge. Manhattan's Annex Antiques Fair and Flea Market is legendary—and open on weekends, all year-round.

# RESOURCE DIRECTORY

Resources are one of the most important aspects of design. There are literally tens of thousands of vendors, artisans, suppliers, manufacturers and retailers out there. In this appendix, you'll find a directory of those listed in the resource sections. Please note that many of the listings have multiple locations. Due to limited space, we've usually included the contact information for the U.S. headquarters only, or where applicable, international headquarters. Call the vendor directly for a location or supplier near you. Also many of the sources listed sell to the trade (architects and designers) only. If you aren't working with an interior designer or architect, see the trade tips section for hints on how to buy trade only merchandise or contact a local design center to see if there's a service that will do so for you.

## Designers

Carl D'Aquino & Francine Monaco
D'Aquino Monaco
180 Varick Street, Fourth Floor
New York, NY 10014
212-929-9787

Joe Nahem
Fox-Nahem Design
82 East 10th Street
New York, NY 10003
212-358-1411
www.foxnahemdesign.com

Elissa Cullman
Cullman & Kravis
790 Madison Avenue
New York, NY 10021
212-249-3874

Ira Grandberg, AIA
Grandberg & Associates
117 Main Street
Mt. Kisco, NY 10549
914-242-0033

Jack Fhillips
Jack Fhillips Design
2611 Mercer Avenue
West Palm Beach, FL 33401
561-659-4459

Glenn Gissler
Glenn Gissler Design
36 East 22nd Street, 8th Floor
New York, NY 10010
212-228-9880

Scott Salvator
308 East 79th Street
New York, NY 10021
212-861-5355

Robert Couturier
69 Mercer Street
New York, NY 10012
212-463-7177

Anthony Ingrao
Ingrao
17 East 64th Street
New York, NY 10021
212-472-5400

Ann LeConey
241 East 78th Street
New York, NY 10021
212-472-1265

Steven R. Gambrel
S.R. Gambrel
270 Lafayette Street, Ste 805
New York, NY 10012
212-925-3380

Randall A. Ridless
315 West 39th Street, Ste 1101
New York, NY 10018
212-643-8140

Peter Chu
Chu/Pettersen Interior Design
75 South Orange Avenue, Ste 206
South Orange, NY 07079
973-762-2886

## Reproduction Furniture

Barbara Berry
Baker Furniture
1661 Monroe Avenue N.W.
Grand Rapids, MI 49505
800-592-2537
www.kohlerinteriors.com

Michael S. Smith
1646 19th Street
Santa Monica, CA 90404
310-315-3018

Randall A. Ridless
315 West 39th Street, Ste 1101
New York, NY 10018
212-643-8140

Frances Mayes
Drexel Heritage Furniture
1925 Eastchester Drive
High Point, N.C. 27265
866-450-3434
www.drexelheritage.com

Martha Stewart
11 West 42nd Street, 25th Floor
New York, NY 10036
888-562-7842
www.marthastewart.com

Michael Kuo
Baker Furniture
1661 Monroe Avenue N.W.
Grand Rapids, MI 49505
800-592-2537
www.kohlerinteriors.com

Julia Gray
D&D Building
979 Third Avenue, Ste 711
New York, NY 10022
212-223-4454

Bill Sofield
Baker Furniture
1661 Monroe Avenue N.W.
Grand Rapids, MI 49505
800-592-2537
www.kohlerinteriors.com

Oscar de la Renta
Century Furniture
P.O. Box 608
Hickory, NC 28603
800-852-5552
www.centuryfurniture.com

Thomas Pheasant
Baker Furniture
1661 Monroe Avenue N.W.
Grand Rapids, MI 49505
800-592-2537
www.kohlerinteriors.com

John Rosselli
523 East 73rd Street
New York, NY 10021
212-772-2137

## Antiques

Artfact
2 Canal Park
Cambridge, MA 02141
617-252-5020
www.artfact.com

Kentshire Galleries
37 East 12th Street
New York, NY 10003
212-673-6644
www.kentshire.com

Ingrao Gallery
17 East 64th Street
New York, NY 10021
212-472-5400

Fair Trade
P.O. Box 122
Shelburne Falls, MA 01370
866-337-8513
www.fairtradeantiques.com

Coconut Company
131 Greene Street
New York, NY 10012
212-539-1940

Howard Kaplan Antiques
827 Broadway
New York, NY 10003
212-674-1000
www.howardkaplanantiques.com

O'Sullivan Antiques
51 East 10th Street
New York, NY 10003
212-260-8985
www.osullivanantiques.com.

Jourdan Antiques
29 East 10th Street
New York, NY 10003
212-674-4470
www.jourdanantiques.com

Pagoda Red
1714 North Damen
Chicago, IL 60647
773-235-1188
www.pagodared.com

J. Tribble Antiques
764 Miami Circle N.E., Ste 112
Atlanta, GA 30324
888-652-6116
www.jtribbleantiques.com

Maison Gerard
53 East 10th Street
New York, NY 10003
212-674-7611
www.maisongerard.com

Broadway Antique Market
6130 North Broadway
Chicago, IL 60660
773-743-5444
www.bamchicago.com

Lafayette Antiques at the Warehouse
401 East 110th Street, 8th Floor
New York, NY 10029
212-722-8400
www.lafayetteantiques.com

Hiden Galleries
481 Canal Street
Stamford, CT 06902
203-323-9090
www.hiden-galleries-antiques.com

The Antique & Artisan Center
69 Jefferson Street
Stamford, CT 06902
203-327-6022
www.stamfordantiquescenter.com

Harbor View Center for Antiques
101 Jefferson Street
Stamford, CT 06902
203-325-8070
www.harborviewantiques.net

Shippan Center for Arts & Antiques
614 Shippan Avenue
Stamford, CT 06902
203-353-0222
www.shippancenter.com

Debbie's Stamford Antiques Center
735 Canal Street
Stamford, CT 06902
888-329-3546

## Antique Furniture and Hand-Painted Furniture

Eli Rios
ECR Antique Conservation and Restoration
515 W 29th Street, Ste 5
New York, NY 10001
866-643-0388
www.ecrios.com

Joseph Biunno
129 West 29th Street
New York, NY 10001
212-629-5630
www.antiquefurnitureusa.com

Swedish Country
D&D Building
979 Third Avenue, Ste 1409
New York, NY 10022
212-838-1976
www.countryswedish.com

Julia Gray
D&D Building
979 Third Avenue, Ste 711
New York, NY 10022
212-223-4454

Decorative Crafts
50 Chestnut Street
Greenwich, CT 06830
800-431-4455
www.decorativecrafts.com

Auffray
200 Lexington Avenue
New York, NY 10016
212-889-4646
www.auffray.com

## Architectural Salvage

Olde Good Things
124 West 24th Street
New York, NY 10011
212-989-8401
www.oldegoodthings.com

Architecturals.net
Urban Development Corporation
PMB 154
12 W. Willow Grove Avenue
Philadelphia, PA 19118
800-658-5096
www.architecturals.net

The Demolition Depot
216 East 125th Street
New York, NY 10035
212-860-1138
www.demolitiondepot.com

Paris Ceramics
150 East 58th Street, 7th Floor
New York, NY 10155
212-644-2782
www.parisceramics.com

Pioneer Millworks
1180 Commercial Drive
Farmington, NY 14425
800-951-9663
www.pioneermillworks.com

Cornerstone
499 Van Brunt Street, Warehouse 8A
Brooklyn, NY 11231
718-855-2673
www.cornerstonesalvage.com

Howard Kaplan Antiques
827 Broadway
New York, NY 10003
212-674-1000
www.howardkaplanantiques.com

Architectural Artifacts
4325 North Ravenswood
Chicago, IL 60613
773-348-0622
www.architecturalartifacts.com

Fair Trade
P.O. Box 122
Shelburne Falls, MA 01370
866-337-8513
www.fairtradeantiques.com

United House Wrecking
535 Hope Street
Stamford, CT 06906
203-348-5371
www.unitedhousewrecking.com

Historic Houseparts
540 South Avenue
Rochester, NY 14620
888-558-2329
www.historichouseparts.com

Old House Parts Company
24 Blue Wave Mall
Kennebunk, Maine 04043
207-985-1999
www.oldhouseparts.com

## Walls

Anthony Lombardo
Architectural Paneling
D&D Building
979 Third Avenue, Ste 919
New York, NY 10022
212-371-9632
www.apaneling.com

Tania Vartan
P.O. Box 2432
Palm Beach, FL 33480
561-827-4848
www.taniavartan.com

Chuck Fischer
32 Union Square East, Ste 1017
New York, NY 10003
212-529-4953

Balmer Architectural Mouldings
271 Yorkland Blvd.
Toronto, ON, M2J 1S5
Canada
800-665-3454
www.balmer.com

Gracie Studios
419 Lafayette Street
New York, NY 10003
212-924-6816
www.graciestudio.com

Designers Guild
Sold in US through:
Osborne & Little
D&D Building
979 Third Avenue, Ste 520
New York, NY 10022
212-751-3333
www.designersguild.com

Stark Wallcoverings
D&D Building
979 Third Avenue, Ste 1101
New York, NY 10022
212-355-7186
www.dir-dd.com/
stark-wallcovering.html

Zoffany
D&D Building
979 3rd Avenue, Ste 1403
New York, NY 10022
800-395-8760
www.zoffany.com

Waverly
79 Madison Avenue
New York, NY 10016
212-213-7900
www.waverly.com

Benjamin Moore
51 Chestnut Ridge Road
Montvale, NJ 07645
800-344-0400
www.benjaminmoore.com

Donald Kaufman Color
336 West 37th Street, Ste 801
New York, NY 10018
212-594-2608
www.donaldkaufmancolor.com

Farrow & Ball
1054 Yonge Street
Toronto, ON M4W 2L1
Canada
888-511-1121
www.farrow-ball.com

Pratt & Lambert Paint
101 Prospect Avenue W
Cleveland, OH 44115
800-289-7728
www.prattandlambert.com

Dunn-Edwards
4885 East 52nd Place
Los Angeles, CA 90040
888-337-2468
www.dunnedwards.com

Schreuder
Sold in US through:
Fine Paints of Europe
P.O. Box 419
Woodstock, VT 05091
800-332-1556
www.finepaintsofeurope.com

Old Fashioned Milk Paint
436 Main Street
Groton, MA 01450
866-350-6455
www.milkpaint.com

## Light Fixtures

Daniel Berglund
141 Grassy Hill Road
Lyme, CT 06371
860-434-5162

Patricia Moore
Gates Moore
5 River Road
Norwalk, CT 06850
203-847-3231
www.gatesmoorelighting.com

Urban Archaeology
143 Franklin Street
New York, NY 10013
212-431-4646
www.urbanarchaeology.com

145 Antiques
145 West 22nd Street
New York, NY 10010
212-807-1149
www.145antiques.com

Lampworks
231 East 58th Street
New York, NY 10022
888-526-7967
www.lampworksinc.com

Oriental Lamp Shade Co.
816 Lexington Avenue
New York, NY 10021
212-832-8190
www.orientallampshade.com

Chameleon
223 East 59th Street
New York, NY 10022
212-355-6300
www.chameleonsoho.com

Charles Edwards
582 King's Road
London SW62DY
England
+44 (0)20-7736-8490
www.charlesedwards.com

Cristal
201 Railhead Road
Fort Worth, TX 76106
817-626-4041
www.cristal-usa.com

Shades from the Midnight Sun
66 Boulder Trail
Bronxville, NY 10708
914-779-7237

Trans-LUXE
10 Greene Street,
New York, NY 10013
212-925-5863
www.trans-luxe.com

## Window Treatments

The Silk Trading Co.
5900 Blackwelder Street
Culver City, CA 90232
800-854-0396
www.silktrading.com

The Curtain Exchange
3936 Magazine Street
New Orleans, LA 70115
504-897-2444
www.thecurtainexchange.com

Hartmann & Forbes
26100 SW 95th Avenue, Ste 200
Wilsonville, OR 97070
888-582-8780
www.hfshades.com

Horizon Shutters
1348 S. Devon Road
Springfield, MO 65809
www.horizonshutters.com
888-399-4947

Hunter Douglas
2 Parkway
Upper Saddle River, NJ 07458
www.hunterdouglas.com
800-937-7895

Joseph Biunno
129 West 29th Street
New York, NY 10011
212-629-5630
www.antiquefurnitureusa.com

Desiron
151 Wooster Street
New York, NY 10012
212-353-2600
www.desiron.com

Finials by John Ragsdale
Department 1
557 Savannah Highway
Charleston, SC 29407
843-766-4114
www.ragsdalefinials.com

M&J Trimming
1008 Sixth Avenue
New York, NY 10018
212-842-5050
www.mjtrim.com

Samuel & Sons
983 Third Avenue
New York, NY 10022
212-704-8000
www.samuelandsons.com

Clarence House
D&D Building
979 Third Avenue
New York, NY 10022
800-221-4704
www.clarencehouse.com

## Textiles

Ed Rollins & Chris Isles
Pintura
207 East 4th Street
New York, NY 10009
212-995-8655

Kazumi Yoshida
Clarence House
D& D Building
979 Third Avenue
New York, NY 10022
800-221-4704
www.clarencehouse.com

Brunschwig & Fils
D&D Building
979 Third Avenue, Ste 1200
New York, NY 10022
212-838-7878
www.brunschwigfils.com

Kime
Available through:
John Rosselli
D&D Building
979 Third Avenue, Ste 1800
New York, NY 10022
212-593-2060

Cora Ginsburg
19 East 74th Street
New York, NY 10021
212-744-1352
www.coraginsburg.com

Schumacher
D&D Building
979 Third Avenue, Ste 832
New York, NY 10022
212-415-3900
www.fschumacher.com

Old World Weavers
D&D Building
979 Third Avenue, Ste 1001
New York, NY 10022
212-752-9000
www.old-world-weavers.com

A.M. Collections
584 Broadway, Ste 806
New York, NY 10012
212- 625-2616

Silk Surplus
942 Third Avenue
New York, NY 10022
212-753-6511
Also see: www.baranzelli.com

Maison Décor
2 Lewis Court
Greenwich, CT 06830
203-422-0440
www.maisondecor.info

## Flooring

Lucretia Moroni
Fatto a Mano
127 Madison Avenue, 4th Floor
New York, NY 10016
212-686-4848
www.fatto-a-mano.com

Artistic Tile
79 Fifth Avenue
New York, NY 10003
800-260-8646
www.artistictile.com

Pioneer Millworks
1180 Commercial Drive
Farmington, NY 14425
800-951-9663
www.pioneermillworks.com

Patina Old World Flooring
3820 North Ventura Avenue
Ventura, CA 93001
800-501-1113
www.patinafloors.com

Country Floors
15 East 16th Street
New York, NY 10003
800-311-9995
www.countryfloors.com

Ann Sacks
1210 S.E Grand Avenue
Portland, OR 97214
800-278-8453
www.annsacks.com

Paris Ceramics
150 East 58th Street, 7th Floor
New York, NY 10155
212-644-2782
www.parisceramics.com

Peacock Pavers
P.O. Box 519
Atmore, AL 36504
800-264-2072
www.peacockpavers.com

## Carpets

Sarah Gayle Carter Studio
107 East Cary Street
Richmond, VA 23219
804-648-7877
www.sarahgaylecarter.com

The Rug Company
88 Wooster Street
New York, NY 10012
212-274-0444
www.therugcompany.info

FJ Hakimian
136 East 57th Street
New York, NY 10022
212-371-6900
www.fjhakimian.com

Stark Carpet
D&D Building
979 Third Avenue, Ste 1101
New York, NY 10022
212-752-9000
www.starkcarpet.com

Abraham Moheban & Sons Antique Carpets
139 East 57th Street
New York, NY 10022
212-758-3900
www.moheban.com

Odegard
200 Lexington Avenue, Ste 1206
New York, NY 10016
800-670-8836
www.odegardinc.com

The Odegard Warehouse
47-14 32nd Place
Long Island City, NY 11101
800-670-8836

Renaissance Carpet & Tapestries
200 Lexington Avenue
New York, NY 10016
800-325-7847
www.renaissancecarpet.com

Asmara
88 Black Falcon Avenue
Boston, MA 02210
800-451-7240
www.asmarainc.com

Schumacher
D&D Building
979 Third Avenue, Ste 832
New York, NY 10022
212-415-3900
www.fschumacher.com

Karastan
508 East Morris Street
Dalton, GA 30721
800-234-1120
www.karastan.com

## Hardware

Carl Martinez Hardware
83 Canal Street
New York, NY 10002
212-941-8142
www.carlmartinezhardware.com

P.E. Guerin
23 Jane Street
New York, NY 10014
212-243-5270
www.peguerin.com

Restoration Hardware
104 Challenger Drive
Portland, TN 37148
800-762-1005
www.restorationhardware.com

Nanz
20 Vandam Street
New York, NY 10013
212-367-7000
www.nanz.com

Whitechapel
P.O. Box 11719
Jackson, WY 83002
307-739-9478
www.whitechapel-ltd.com

Crown City Hardware
1047 North Allen Avenue
Pasadena, CA 91140
800-950-1047
www.restoration.com

The Old House Store
Hampstead Farm
Binfield Heath
Oxfordshire RG9 4LG
England
+44 (0)11-8969-6949
www.oldhousestore.co.uk

House of Antique Hardware
3439 N.E. Sandy Boulevard
P.M.B. #106
Portland, OR 97232
888-223-2545
www.houseofantiquehardware.com

Elliott's Hardware
4901 Maple Avenue
Dallas, TX 75235
214-634-9900
www.elliottshardware.com

Rejuvenation
2550 N.W. Nicolai Street
Portland, Oregon 97210
888-401-1900
www.rejuvenation.com

Van Dyke Restorers
P.O. Box 278
Woonsocket, S.D. 57385
800-558-1234
www.vandykes.com

Joseph Biunno
129 West 29th Street
New York, NY 10011
212-629-5630
www.antiquefurnitureusa.com

## Accessories

Simon Pearce
Route 5
P.O. Box 1
Windsor, VT 05089
877-452-7763
www.simonpearce.com

Decorative Crafts
50 Chestnut Street
Greenwich, CT 06830
800-431-4455
www.decorativecrafts.com

Scully & Scully
504 Park Avenue
New York, NY 10022
800-223-3717
www.scullyandscully.com

Alan Moss
436 Lafayette Street
New York, NY 10003
212-473-1310
www.alanmossny.com

Scuola del Cuoio
The Leather School of Florence
Piazza Santa Croce, 16
50122 Florence, Italy
011 39 55 244 533
www.leatherschool.it

Gracious Home
1217 Third Avenue
New York, NY 10021
212-517-6300
www.gracioushome.com

William-Wayne & Co.
850 Lexington Avenue
New York NY 10021
800-318-3435
www.william-wayne.com

Skyscraper
237 East 60th Street
New York, NY 10022
212-588-0644
www.skyscraperny.com

Deco Deluxe II
1038 Lexington Avenue
New York, NY 10021
212-249-5066
www.skyscraper.com

Carole Stupell
29 East 22nd Street
New York, NY 10010
212-260-3100

J. Pocker & Sons
D&D Building
979 Third Avenue, Ste 900
New York, NY 10022
212-588-0043
800-443-3116
www.jpocker.com

Lyons Ltd. Antique Prints
10 Town and Country Village
Palo Alto, CA 94301
800-596-6758
www.lyonsltdantiqueprints.com

## Plumbing

DeeDee Gundberg
Ann Sacks
8120 N.E. 33rd Drive
Portland, OR 97211
800-278-8453
www.annsacks.com

Waterworks
60 Backus Avenue
Danbury, CT 06810
800-899-6757
www.waterworks.com

P.E. Guerin
23 Jane Street
New York, NY 10014
212-243-5270
www.peguerin.com

Artistic Tile
79 Fifth Avenue
New York, NY 10003
800-260-8646
www.artistictile.com

Herbeau
3600 Westview Drive
Naples, Fl 34104
239-417-5368
www.herbeau.com

Lefroy Brooks USA
16 Crosby Street
New York, NY 10013
212-226-2242
www.lefroybrooks.com

Urban Archaeology
143 Franklin Street
New York, NY 10013
212-431-4646
www.urbanarchaeology.com

Kallista
44 Highland Drive, Mailstop 032
Kohler, WI 53044
888-452-5547
www.kallistainc.com

Renaissance Tile and Bath
349 Peachtree Hills Avenue N.E.
Atlanta, GA 30305
800-275-1822
www.renaissancetileandbath.com

Kohler
444 Highland Drive
Kohler, WI 53044
800-456-4537
www.kohler.com

## Trade Tips

Ira Grandberg, AIA
Grandberg & Associates
117 Main Street
Mt. Kisco, NY 10549
914-242-0033

Ellen S. Fisher, ASID
New York School of Interior Design
170 East 70th Street
New York, NY 10021
212-472-1500

Karen Fisher
Designer Previews
36 Gramercy Park East
New York, NY 10003
212-777-2966
www.designerpreviews.com

The Franklin Guide
866-990-9100
www.franklinreport.com

HomePortfolio
288 Walnut Street, Ste 200
Newton, MA 02460
617-965-0565
www.homeportfolio.com

Lin Walters
Design Professionals
D&D Building
979 Third Avenue, Ste 1400
New York, NY 10022
212-759-6894
www.ddbuilding.com

Izolli Home Collection
29020 Agoura Road
Agoura Hills, CA 91301
800-772-1343
www.izolli.com

Decorator's Secret
1735 Canal Street
Building 19
Stamford, CT 06902
203-323-5093
www.thedecoratorssecret.com

Connecticut Trading Co
72 Old Ridgefield Rd
Wilton, CT 06897
203-834-5008

Silk Purse
118 Main St
New Canaan, CT 06840
203-972-0898

Marston House
101 Main Street
Wiscasset, ME 04578
207-882-6010
www.marstonhouse.com

Pumpkin Patch Antiques
15 West Main Street
Searsport, Maine 04974
207-548-6047

Annex Antiques Fair and Flea Market
P.O. Box 7010
New York, NY 10016
212-243-5343

# INDEX

## PHOTOGRAPHY CREDITS

**QUENTIN BACON**
**212-868-0332**
164

**ANDREW BORDWIN**
**212-529-4953**
70-79 (all), 154 (2)

**ROBERT BRANTLEY**
**516-265-0995**
10 (bottom, middle)

**BRUCE BUCK**
**212-645-1022**
46-49 (all)

**MEREDITH CURTS**
**917-374-9221**
Author photo

**PETER D'APRIX**
125 (5,6)

**TIM M. EBERT**
**718-558-6806**
84-90 (all), 91 (top), 94 (2), 108 (3,4)

**SCOTT FRANCIS**
**212-227-2722**
107

**ALISON GOOGEE**
**404-314-8339**
150 (2)

**H/O PHOTOGRAPHERS**
**802-295-6321**
154 (4)

**LIZZIE HIMMEL**
**212-683-5331**
12-21 (all), 94 (3), 154 (1), 190

**PAUL HORTON PHOTOGRAPHY**
38 (1), 54 (3)

**THIBAULT JEANSON**
**212-682-1490**
105

**ROBERT A. KERN**
**201-791-9355**
24 (1)

**LAURIE LAMBRECHT**
**212-534-0188**
8, 165

**HEATHER LASZLO**
**212-663-1990**
140-149 (all)

**ROBERT LEVIN**
38 (2,3)

**DEBORAH WHITLAW LLEWELLYN**
**404-525-3535**
Front cover, 56-65 (all)

**JOAN MARCUS**
**212-529-4953**
67 (5,6), 111 (3)

**PETER MARGONELLI**
**212-431-5494**
11 (bottom, right)

**GEORGE MOTT**
11 (bottom, middle)

**GEORGE OBREMSKI**
**212-684-2933**
11 (top, middle)

**LAURA RESEN**
**917-374-4467**
Back cover, 4-5, 11 (bottom, right), 26-35 (all), 98, 102, 103, 104, 172-181(all)

**PIERO RIBELLI**
111 (1), 122 (all)

**LAURA COHEN RONICK**
10 (top, middle)

**KIM SARGENT**
**561-881-8887**
126-134 (all)

**DURSTON SAYLOR**
**212-779-3901**
1, 40-45 (all), 108 (1,2)

**JONATHON SHOWS**
10 (top, right)

**DAVID LEWIS TAYLOR**
**212-647-8727**
158-136 (all), 166, 167, 191-192

**LAURENCE VETA-GALUD**
6, 100, 106

**CHRISTOPHER WESNOFSKE**
**212-529-4953**
3, 112-121 (all)

All other photos courtesy of designer or manufacturer.